POCKET
BONSAI

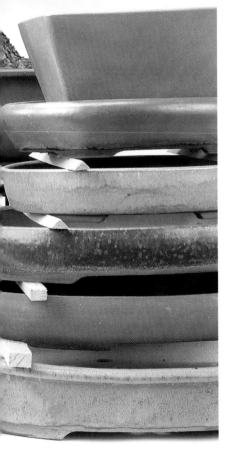

POCKET
BONSAI

David Prescott

CONSULTANT EDITOR COLIN LEWIS

NEW
HOLLAND

HALF TITLE *The trunk of this miniature bonsai, or* mame, *displays natural curves.*

FULL TITLE *Simple containers and implements are employed in the practice of the complex and deeply satisfying art form that is bonsai.*

TOP *A selection of the tools used in bonsai, ranging from ordinary household items to a few highly specialized implements.*

OPPOSITE *This ancient Japanese painting shows that the art of bonsai has been practised in the East for many centuries.*

NEW
HOLLAND

First Published in 2004 by New Holland Publishers
London • Cape Town • Sydney • Auckland
www.newholland publishers.com

86 Edgware Road, London W2 2EA, United Kingdom.
80 McKenzie Street, Cape Town 8001, South Africa,
14 Aquatic Drive, Frenchs Forest, NSW 2086, Australia.
218 Lake Road, Northcote Auckland, New Zealand.

ISBN 1 84330 586 0

Publisher Mariëlle Renssen
Publishing managers Claudia dos Santos, Simon Pooley
Designer and studio manager Richard MacArthur
Editors Romi Bryden, Gill Gordon
Illustrations Steven Felmore
Picture researcher Sonya Meyer, Karla Kik
Indexer Gill Gordon
Production Myrna Collins
Consultants Dr Malcolm Hughes (UK),
Dr Carl Morrow (SA)

Reproduction by Unifoto Pty Ltd
Printed and bound in Singapore by Kyodo Printing Co.
10 9 8 7 6 5 4 3

CONTENTS

Foreword   9

Introduction   11

Science or art?   17

The art of bonsai   31

Your own bonsai collection   43

Keeping your bonsai alive   53

Keeping your bonsai healthy   65

Keeping your bonsai in shape   77

Repotting   105

Growing your own bonsai   119

Starting work   143

Directory   161

Glossary   188

Index   190

Credits and acknowledgements   192

LEFT Shade netting allows light to filter gently through to the trees, while protecting vulnerable ones from the more harmful ultraviolet rays of the sun.

FOREWORD

The essence of bonsai

Although bonsai is an ancient oriental art, it is just as relevant to today's Western culture as it was in the East, when it originated in China over 2000 years ago.

People everywhere have always had an affinity with nature, and people everywhere feel the urge to represent these things in the form of art; in painting, poetry, music and sculpture. In this high-tech era, this kind of empathy with our natural surroundings is even more important, helping us relax and unwind. What better way do this, and to pay homage to mother nature's most magnificent creations, than through the venerable art of bonsai?

The principles of bonsai are simple to learn and very easy to apply. For example, we all keep plants in pots, on our balconies, patios and even in our living rooms; there's nothing new about that. We prune our shrubs, clip our hedges and fashion some plants into the recognizable shapes of birds or animals. Nothing new there either!

The only thing that makes bonsai different from any other form of horticulture is that it involves creating a miniature image of a larger tree, and keeping it that way, in a container that is shallower than usual. The only thing that makes it different from any other art form, is that the medium we work with is alive and constantly changing.

Bonsai involves no magic potions, no special philosophy, and no degree in oriental studies. All it requires is a woody plant, a pot, a handful of basic tools, and a few years' patience. Think you can manage that? Of course!

When David Prescott first came to me to study bonsai, I recognized at once his innate talent and burning passion for the art. Since then, he has studied with many of Europe's leading experts and has become a master in his own right. His down-to-earth approach and his unfailing sympathy with the worries and uncertainties of the absolute beginner have made him a very popular teacher.

Here, he not only brings to you his deep knowledge of the subject, but does so in a way that makes bonsai seem so easy that you wonder why people make such a fuss.

Read this book, try out the techniques for yourself (if you kill a few trees, don't worry – we've all done that!). Above all, have fun – that's what bonsai is all about.

Sincerely,

Colin Lewis

OPPOSITE *The art of bonsai*
involves creating a miniature of a larger tree and maintaining it in a shallow pot.

INTRODUCTION

What is bonsai?

Bonsai, literally translated, means tree-in-a-pot. This, however, is a broad definition which needs qualification. Perhaps it would be easier to explain what bonsai is not. A bonsai is neither a dwarf variety, nor is it a tree miniaturized by means of magic. Keeping the roots confined in a pot assists with mobility and allows for a unified composition, but that is not what keeps a bonsai small and beautiful, either. The size, shape and attractiveness of a bonsai is entirely dependent upon its owner's dedication to its daily care and his or her taste and artistic ability.

Nobody knows when the idea first arose that one could shape trees in containers to mimic their full-sized counterparts. There is clear evidence that the Chinese were doing it over 2000 years ago. Paintings of that period depict shallow pots with trees and rocks, which look like landscapes in miniature. However, it was the Japanese who took up, refined and developed the practice.

HISTORY OF BONSAI

Throughout history, much of Japanese culture and art came under Chinese influence. The Japanese script even uses the same characters for the word bonsai as does the Chinese script. But, over the past few centuries, these two ancient cultures have moved further and further apart and, as in so many other spheres, this is reflected in their different approach to bonsai.

In China, most bonsai (pronounced 'punsai'), or penjing, include elements of landscape. The trees themselves may appear to imitate animals, and those with bizarre, unnatural-looking shapes and exposed roots are often the most highly prized.

The Japanese, on the other hand, have simplified the bonsai image, distilling it to its basic elements. They have refined both the artistic and horticultural aspects of bonsai culture to such an extent that they have set almost impossibly high standards for the rest of the world to follow. Certain classic styles have been defined, based on the attitudes of the trunks. The ideal positions of branches, the proportions of the trees, shape of the trunks, and the relationship between the plant and its container, have all been perfected by Japanese bonsai growers.

OPPOSITE *Bonsai trees are sometimes displayed in creative ways to mimic trees in their natural environment. This Japanese White Pine* (Pinus parviflora), *seemingly growing on a hill, is actually a 100-year-old miniature specimen.*

The first major exhibitions of bonsai trees were held in Japan in the early 1900s. This was a turning point for the development of bonsai. For the first time, wealthy patrons of the arts and members of the public came together to acknowledge the artistic value of the bonsai. As a result of these exhibitions, the number of professional bonsai growers in Japan increased dramatically.

In the 1920s, a devastating earthquake destroyed a large proportion of the bonsai growing area on the island of Hokkaido. Vast numbers of trees were lost and many of Japan's most accomplished practitioners perished. However, with typical Japanese determination, a handful of survivors founded a bonsai village in Omiya, on the outskirts of Tokyo, where they began once more to cultivate the attractive miniature trees.

Today, Omiya has been almost absorbed by the vast urban sprawl of Tokyo's suburbs, but some of the original bonsai nurseries are still there, many of them owned by descendants of the founding masters.

Other countries in the Far East also have centuries-old traditions of bonsai culture. Korea, Vietnam, Taiwan and Indonesia have developed recognizable national styles. The stylistic distinctions are, as often as not, the result of differences in climate. Each climatic zone has its own species of trees and the different growth patterns, individual responses to training techniques, and the natural forms

ABOVE *This hardy European Hornbeam* (Carpinus betalus) *takes on a magic all of its own when the first snow has fallen in winter.*

unique to each species, all influence the final image a grower is able to produce.

Other factors that influence the emergence of national or regional styles include religion, artistic heritage, economics and social structures. In countries where the standard of living is generally high, the bonsai are larger, more lush and more refined. But where much of the population spends most of its waking hours at work, the bonsai are more modest.

Bonsai is not a hobby only for the rich and leisured, but it does involve some expense, and demands considerable time and commitment

if one is to be successful. Bonsai is not a static art. In spite of the quite-rigorous criteria of the classical practice, there is much creative potential on offer to the imaginative artist with a green thumb.

Several new classical styles have become accepted as old traditions slowly give way to change, and the development of modern techniques enables growers to do things which were previously impossible. One thing, however, will endure, and that is the feeling of joy that arises from contemplating the living work of art that is a bonsai masterpiece.

TOP *In this old Japanese painting, well-dressed ladies are depicted in an elegant garden setting. On the left of the garden room, bonsai trees are displayed in porcelain pots. The bonsai echo the full-size tree in bloom outside, at the edge of the tranquil lake.*

▸ THE HOBBY TODAY ◂

The practice of growing and shaping trees in containers was carried out in Europe in the 18th century, but there is no evidence to suggest that this was done for decorative purposes. It was more likely to have had a practical origin, in that favourite fruit trees could be more easily transported from house to house by itinerant merchants.

Bonsai from Japan and China first appeared in Europe at an exhibition in Paris towards the end of the 19th century. The little trees turned up in London soon after that and history records that auctions of specially imported bonsai were held there prior to World War I. Those plants were not long-lived because no one knew how to care for them properly and the hobby initially failed to capture the imagination of the public.

Merchants and diplomats returning from the East would occasionally bring trees home. There are still some Hinoki Cypresses (*Chamaecyparis obtusa*) in the USA that formed part of a venerable collection brought back by Larz Anderson, a former American ambassador to Japan. Among these ancient bonsai are some with a recorded history dating back to the early 1800s, and they are still going strong.

It was not until after World War II that the art of bonsai began to achieve popular recognition worldwide. Servicemen returned home with memories and, sometimes, one or two examples of these fascinating little trees. Gradually, people began to learn more about them, how to keep them in good condition, how to shape and train them and, best of all, how to create them from scratch.

ABOVE *A well laid-out modern bonsai nursery in Omiya, Japan, where trees are developed and refined before being offered for sale.*

Among the expatriate Japanese population of California who helped spread the word was John Yoshio Naka, who achieved such renown in both the USA and in Japan that he was granted one of the Emperor's highest awards for his services in sustaining and promoting the respected art of bonsai.

Western bonsai enthusiasts began to band together, and by the 1970s most countries had thriving clubs. Enterprising nurseries began importing trees from Japan. In those days they were much more expensive than today, but were frequently better specimens as well. Nowdays bonsai are mass-produced for export in such enormous volumes that both price and (unfortunately) quality have declined.

Trees of excellence, once formerly exported by Japanese owners who were delighted that their work was so admired in the West, are now reserved for serious domestic collectors. Western enthusiasts who want a top specimen bonsai tree have either to create it themselves, or purchase one produced by local growers.

Some Western bonsai artists produce work that is much admired in Japan. The repetition and conservatism that characterize so much of Japanese culture have led to a vast understanding of how trees function and how best to train them. But these traditional traits have also served to discourage experimentation.

Western culture, on the other hand, tends to promote progress: making your own rules and doing your own thing are encouraged. Exciting developments are possible when such freedom is creatively applied to the art of bonsai. One day, perhaps, Japanese bonsai masters may come under the influence of their Western counterparts and begin to expand the artistic frontiers of their own work.

Bonsai is now an established pastime throughout the world. Mass-produced, so-called bonsai are sold in supermarkets and florists all over; and clubs and national and international associations organize popular events and exhibitions that are well-attended. Specialist nurseries abound, where trees, pots, tools, soil, everything the enthusiast could want, can be bought at half the price one would have had to pay 20 years ago.

However, despite attempts by mass growers to lower the price of ready-made bonsai in order to satisfy the market, there is nothing that can rival the satisfaction of growing your own. Whether you start with a seedling or an ancient tree rescued from a lost garden, the intimacy of working with nature to create a thing of great beauty has a profound effect on the soul. Enjoy it to the full.

TOP *An expert practitioner conducting a workshop for an enthusiastic group dedicated to the practice of a venerable and ancient art.*

ABOVE *Exhibits at the famous Kokufu Ten bonsai exhibition which attracts well over 20,000 visitors to Tokyo each February.*

BONSAI

Science or art?

It is sometimes asked whether bonsai is simply a horticultural discipline that requires an understanding of how trees function and how they respond to external factors, or whether it is an artistic challenge to use an ever-changing medium to create an object of beauty. Ideally, it combines the two: it satisfies the basic human need to commune with nature and the creative urge that lies within us all.

▶ ANATOMY OF A BONSAI ◀

The roots

We take it for granted that all plants have roots of one kind or another but, if we are going to be responsible for keeping a tree alive and in the best of health, it is essential that we understand a little more about its roots.

The function of roots Roots have three primary functions. The first is, quite simply, to stop a tree from falling over. The roots that spread out from the base of any tree trunk extend in all directions, anchoring the tree in the soil. This applies equally to bonsai. If a bonsai is easily rocked in its pot, then the roots are failing and, if the roots are weak, the tree will also be weak.

The second function of roots is to draw nutrients and water from the soil. Species that are adapted to grow in arid regions have long, searching roots which tap moisture from a wide area. Those that live in moist, fertile soil have fine, shallow roots that may not extend beyond the spread of branches. A tree living in the confines of a bonsai pot must have a well-developed, efficient root system to stay healthy.

The third function of roots is to act as a pantry for the tree. During the dormant season, the roots store the sugars that were manufactured by the leaves throughout the summer months. A tree's storage areas are in its heavy, woody roots, so it is vital to develop and preserve an adequate number of these sturdy roots on your bonsai.

OPPOSITE *Adventitious buds which have generated randomly in response to damage.*
ABOVE *One of the main functions of roots is to anchor a tree firmly in the soil.*

How roots work If you examine the roots of a tree or shrub, even on a small nursery plant, you'll notice that there is no taproot. The taproot is the first root produced by a seedling; it grows directly downward to seek out moisture while it provides stability. People used to think that the taproot continued to extend downward for a considerable distance, but that is now known not to be the case. Roots will only grow down as deeply as they need to locate a constant supply of water and, in most cases, that is not very deep.

It is worth noting that a trees' roots are structured rather like branches; the thickest roots radiate outwards from the base of the trunk, they then fork regularly and terminate in masses of fine roots at the tips. In a full-sized tree, these fine feeding roots may be located way beyond the outer reaches of the branches and can cover a massive area.

CROSS-SECTION THROUGH A SIDE ROOT

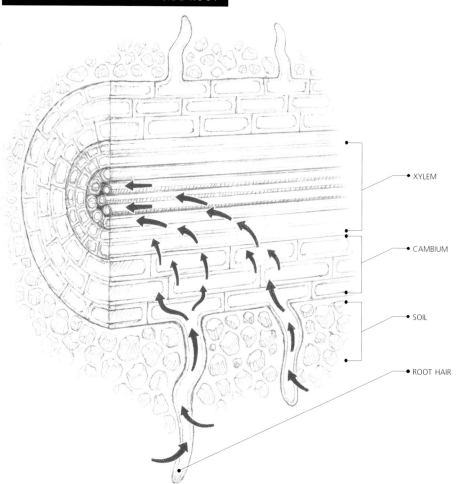

XYLEM

CAMBIUM

SOIL

ROOT HAIR

ABOVE *The finest single-cell root hairs absorb water and nutrients from the soil and distribute them throughout the tree.*

In a bonsai tree, however, the roots don't have the luxury of wide open spaces. They must be super-efficient and able to gather all that the tree requires to keep it in good health from a relatively small volume of soil. To do this effectively, the majority of the roots should be encouraged to become very fine and dense in close proximity to the trunk.

Moisture is drawn into the plant for absorption by osmosis, first and foremost via the finest of fine root hairs, single-cell outgrowths that occur all along the length of the growing tips of the fine roots. In some cases, root hairs are so minute as to be impossible to see without the use of a magnifying glass, while in others they are large and long enough to be

ABOVE *These nebari, or thick roots, anchor the tree in the soil and act as pantries for the plants by storing sugars over the winter months.*
TOP *A thick taproot and a mesh of finer side roots on a young plant. The taproot is the first root to develop on a seedling; it provides anchorage and seeks moisture.*

noticeable. The process of osmosis is a simple one and is worth investigation at this point.

Osmosis – a fair exchange

The walls of the root hairs are permeable, that is to say, water molecules are able to pass through them. The fluid inside the cells of the root hairs is packed with a high concentration of nutrients in the form of mineral salts, while the water on the outside of the cells contains a much lower concentration. In order to balance the two, water passes from the moist soil through the cell walls and into the root hairs, in effect, causing the dilution of the concentration of mineral salts contained within the root. As the water passes through

TOP *A sturdy set of aerial roots on a Banyan Fig* (Ficus retusa), *which makes for a particularly effective bonsai in the Root-over-Rock Style.*

the cell wall it carries with it the nutrients it is holding in solution.

If the concentration of nutrients in the soil is higher than that within the roots (for example, if you have given your tree more than the recommended dose of fertilizer), water will pass from the roots back into the soil and the roots will die of dehydration. This is what gardeners call 'root burn', and it explains why smart gardeners allow farmyard manure to stand and rot for about a year before applying it to the soil.

The thicker roots act as winter storage vessels for the sugars that the leaves have produced during the summer months.

In late summer, the sugars are passed down to the roots for storage, and remain there until the buds begin to swell again in the following spring. At this point, the fine roots begin to take on water to pump into the swelling buds.

As the water is passed upwards through the roots and into the trunk, it facilitates the growth of new shoots and leaves. Once the new leaves are properly established, they are able to support themselves fully and the growth cycle begins all over again.

Healthy roots mean healthy trees

The experienced bonsai grower knows that if a tree looks seedy, it is likely to have something to do with the roots. It might be that they are growing in an environment that is either too wet or too dry, or they may have been damaged by frost or by insect larvae. Also, the roots may have been over-fed; or perhaps they are not able to gather enough good nutrients or minerals from poor soil. All these points will be covered in greater depth in later chapters.

A bonsai tree may fail to thrive because the roots are not properly structured. To survive in bonsai pots, trees need short, thick roots for winter storage, and masses of the finest feeding roots with which to gather in moisture and nutrients.

Medium-sized roots that are neither thick enough to be used as storage hampers nor fine enough to feed with should be kept to a minimum. Correct root pruning and excellent soil guarantee a strong, efficient root system and, therefore, a tree that is in peak condition.

ABOVE *The fine roots growing from the thicker ones absorb moisture and nutrients from the soil. Roots of intermediate size are unnecessary on a bonsai tree.*

▸ THE TRUNK AND BRANCHES ◂

Like the roots, the trunk and branches have three functions. They store sugars in the dormant period; act as highways to transport water and nutrients from the roots to the leaves, and energy-rich sugars from the leaves to other parts of the tree; and they ensure the leaves have a high and wide distribution, in order to gain maximum exposure to sunlight.

If you look at a cross-section of a trunk or branch (see below), you'll see the familiar annual rings, each one indicating a year's growth. Fast-growing trees have thick annual rings and slow-growing trees have thin ones. A 100-year-old bonsai with a 5cm (2in) trunk will have annual rings that are no more than 0.25mm (0.09in) wide!

The wood in the centre of the trunk is darker and harder. This is the heartwood, which is dead, it neither stores sugars nor transports water. Heartwood is just structural timber, adding physical strength to the trunk to enable it to support branches. This is why trees which become hollow can still thrive,

CROSS-SECTION THROUGH A TRUNK

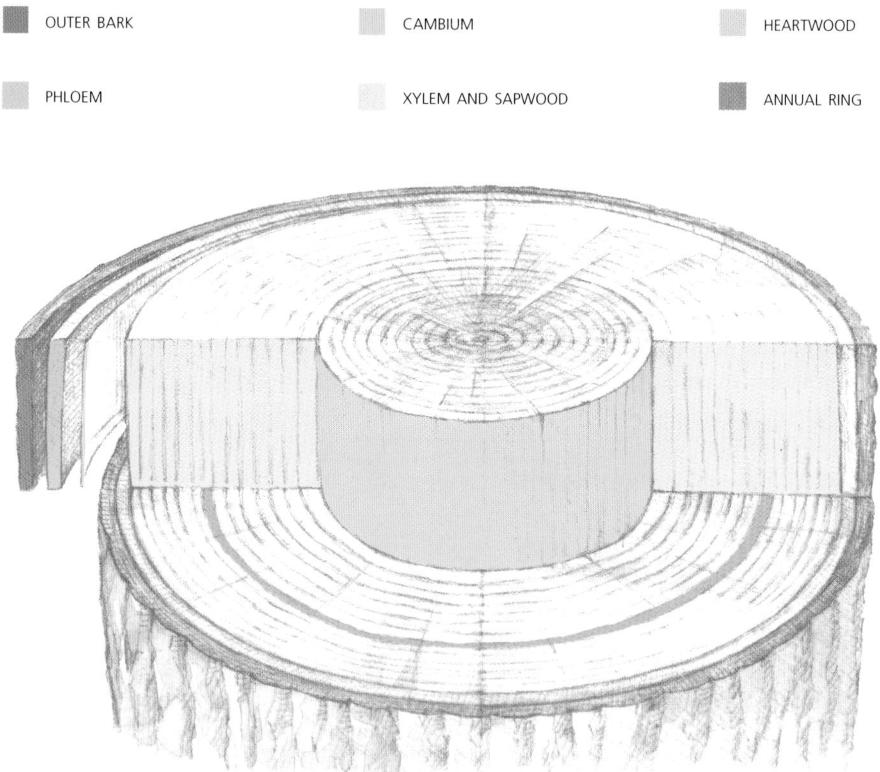

■ OUTER BARK

■ CAMBIUM

■ HEARTWOOD

■ PHLOEM

■ XYLEM AND SAPWOOD

■ ANNUAL RING

ABOVE *Cross-section of a trunk, showing the annual rings of heartwood and sapwood as well as the xylem, cambium, phloem and bark. The lines radiating from the centre are the medullary rays which store up sugars during the dormancy.*

though, naturally, a few do fall down. The paler wood, or sapwood, is also structural, but the outer rings are also involved in the transport of water and nutrients from the roots to the growing parts of the tree: the shoots, leaves, flowers and fruit.

The rings which transport the water and nutrients are called the xylem (pronounced 'zylem'). As xylem ages, it becomes less efficient until it ceases to have any function at all and becomes heartwood.

In winter, the sugars are largely stored in vessels called medullary rays. These rays will radiate through the sapwood from the outer edge of the heartwood.

On the outside of the trunk are two darker, softer layers. The inner layer is the phloem (pronounced 'flo-em'), which distributes sugars from the leaves to the other parts of the tree, giving them energy to grow. If you ringbark a tree (cut a strip of bark away round the trunk), the tree will die. Not because the crown of the tree is starved of water, but because the roots don't get the sugars they need to survive. If you damage the phloem by deep-pruning a branch or allowing training wire to crush the bark, it interrupts the flow of essential sugars. This may lead to the death of the roots below the damaged area. Each year a new layer of phloem is produced, but this doesn't normally lead to the formation of such clearly visible rings as the xylem.

Enveloping the phloem is bark, which varies in thickness and texture according to species. Bark is made up of an accumulation of old, spent phloem, and has a variety of practical purposes. Bark is waterproof, so it prevents moisture from leaking out of the phloem. It is also home to small structures, called lenticels, which permit the trunk and the branches to 'breathe'. Another function that the bark performs is to protect the phloem from impact, abrasions and attack by a variety of insects or fungal infection.

The cambium

Between the xylem and the phloem is what may justly be called the most crucial part of the tree, the cambium. This layer is just one cell thick and shows as a bright green film when the outer 'skin' (the phloem) of a twig is scratched away. In spite of its thinness, the cambium is highly active. Throughout the growing season the cambium cells constantly divide, producing new xylem cells on the inside and new phloem cells on the outside. When winter comes, this process slows almost to a standstill, while a new ring forms.

The cambium is able to adjust its work rate to the growth conditions of the tree. In situations in which a tree can't get sufficient water or nutrients, such as when the tree is confined to a pot, the cambium slows down the rate of cell division.

When a tree is adequately fed and watered, the cambium speeds up, producing thicker annual rings. In bonsai, we are aware that life

ABOVE *These crowded pine candles have arisen in response to consistent pruning.*

in a pot is bound to affect the vigour of a tree, so we must attempt to counterbalance this restriction by creating a very efficient root system and feeding it well.

If the cambium is kept active, the trunk thickens more rapidly, which helps the bark to mature, increasing the tree's value. The cambium is enormously versatile, so much so that it is even able to alter the nature of new cells to perform any number of essential tasks. When grafting, it's vital to get the two foreign cambium layers to meet exactly, because it is these that 'fuse' together. Once fusion has successfully taken place, the new xylem and phloem cells that it produces within the union are able to function as continuous pathways.

If you cut through a branch in summer, you will eventually find a ring of fresh buds crowding around the cut between the wood and bark. These have been developed by the cambium layer, which has modified its function in response to losing the supply of hormones produced by actively growing shoots and buds.

Adventitious buds (ones which are produced at random) growing from the older branches and trunks of trees are also generated by the cambium in response to stress higher up the tree. When cuttings are taken, the cambium generates the roots for the new plant. It also gives rise to new roots during the process known as air-layering.

▸ THE FOLIAGE ◂

The leaves are the food factories of a tree. They take water supplied by the roots, plus carbon dioxide from the atmosphere, and convert them into complex sugars, making use of sunlight to energize the reaction, in a process known as photosynthesis. Sunlight is captured by the green chlorophyll, which acts as a catalyst for the chemical reaction that takes place. Even red-leaved species feature green chlorophyll, but this may be masked by the red pigmentation which is present in greater abundance.

CROSS-SECTION THROUGH A LEAF

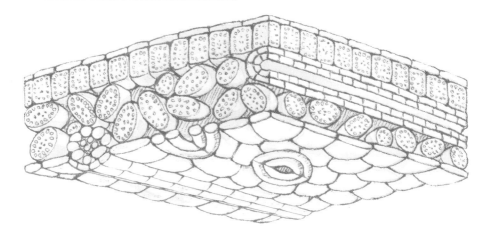

ABOVE *This cross-section through a leaf shows the stomata and the sausage-shaped guard cells that are responsible for opening and closing them.*

During the day, the leaves take in oxygen and carbon dioxide through pores, called stomata, which are usually found on the underside of each leaf. At night they expel carbon dioxide by respiration. The stomata are able to open and close in response to the ambient temperature and humidity, thus controlling the rate at which water evaporates from the leaf. Of necessity, some water has to evaporate all the time in order that a fresh supply of moisture is kept flowing up towards the leaves from the roots.

Leaf shape and size varies tremendously between species. Large, flat leaves capture the maximum amount of light. Narrow pine needles are adapted to be drought resistant. They don't get weighed down with heavy layers of snow, but have a large surface area in comparison with their volume. This way they are still able to capture plenty of light. Some species have waxy leaves in an attempt to prevent excessive evaporation, while others have leaves covered in dense hairs, which achieve the same end.

All leaves have one thing in common: they emerge from buds which form at the tips of shoots (these are called apical buds), often in clusters. On conifers, buds also form at random points along each shoot, of which the precise number and density depends upon the length of the shoot and the vigour of the tree. On broadleaved trees, a bud appears at the base of each leaf stalk (petiole). These buds are called axillary buds.

When pruning or pinching growing shoots on a bonsai, it's important to consider the location of buds because these are the points from which the new shoots will emerge. If the bud faces left, the shoot will grow to the left; if it faces right, then the shoot will bear right.

TOP *Brightly coloured Trident Maple* (Acer buergeranium) *leaves in autumn. Chlorophyll is always green but its colour has been overwhelmed by red pigmentation.*

ABOVE *A miniature Trident Maple (Acer buergeranium) forest without its characteristic foliage, with the buds in their dormant period. Since the buds of all plants are as individual as their leaves, it is as easy to identify them in winter as it is when they are in full leaf.*

▶ BUDS ◀

Buds are miraculous things. Their outer scales are modified leaves whose function is to protect their delicate contents. Inside each mature bud is a tightly packed shoot, complete with its first few leaves, the apical bud and even embryonic axillary buds.

A bud looks just like the inside of a cabbage if it were cut in half vertically (see p29). Imagine the intricacy of an elm bud with all those elements packed into something the size of a pinhead.

Buds vary in character as much as leaves do. In the winter months, buds provide a reliable means of identifying deciduous trees, even without any leaves to go by.

New shoots also vary. Pines, for example, produce vertical shoots, known as candles, which extend rapidly with their tiny needles pressed flat against them. Once they have reached their fullest extent, the needles begin to elongate and peel away from the shoot. Spruce and larch buds, on the other hand, open to reveal tufts of tightly packed, soft needles, which look for all the world like miniature shaving brushes.

During the summer months, the leaves are used to make sugars to nourish the tree's growth but, when eventually the leaves become redundant, they turn brown and fall off.

ABOVE *The buds of two types of deciduous trees: (1) opening maple buds, (2) the buds of an elm, just opening.*

LOCATION OF BUDS

APICAL BUDS DEVELOP ON THE ENDS OF THE SHOOTS,
AXILLARY BUDS AT THE LEAF JOINTS, WHILE THE
ADVENTITIOUS BUDS OCCUR AT RANDOM.

APICAL BUD

AXILLARY BUDS

ADVENTITIOUS BUDS

TOP *The buds of the pine tree, with pine candles extending as they mature.*

In the case of deciduous trees, by their first autumn, the leaves are worn out, whereas the needles (or leaves) of conifers often last for two years, or even longer.

In autumn, the joint between the petiole (leaf stalk) and the shoot seals off in deciduous trees, and the chlorophyll (green colouring) breaks down, allowing the residual pigments to show. This is what causes that brilliant blaze of autumn colour that people who live in temperate zones are privileged to enjoy.

Spectacular autumn colour cannot always be relied upon though. It depends on the health and vigour of the individual trees, as well as the feeding programme that was followed in the preceding summer.

Weather plays a definite role in the development of autumn finery. In wet years, the autumn colours are often poor. However, when the autumn weather is clear with sunny days and frosty nights, the colours produced will be intense.

In nature, nothing can be done about the weather, but with bonsai it is possible to enhance your chances of achieving a spectacular show of the best possible autumn colour by maintaining control over the feeding and watering of your plants.

ABOVE *A cabbage is a perfect illustration of a giant bud which contains a partially developed central shoot, tightly packed leaves and even embryonic axillary buds.*

THE ART
OF BONSAI

Bonsai aesthetics

There is something about a tree that touches one's very soul. This feeling probably dates back to primeval days when early humans relied upon trees for protection, warmth, shelter and food. Where trees were found, there was a potential home. Throughout history, trees have played a major role in primitive religions, and mystical powers have been attributed to them. This strong emotional tie still resides within all of us, and the pleasure that is to be gained from creating and keeping a miniature tree of one's own appeals to a great many people.

In spite of all the horticultural knowledge and practical techniques you may master, bonsai is a visual discipline. It is all about forming an idealized, miniature image of a tree in an imagined natural setting. This could be a graceful lowland maple standing proudly in an open meadow, a forest of elms on a distant hill; or an ancient pine, torn and battered by mountain storms. The possibilities are endless, the horizons limited only by the scope of your own imagination. Nowadays, some artists go way beyond the accepted image of the tree and create abstract, living sculptures, with a mass of swirling deadwood interlaced with foliage. But, to those brave souls prepared to take the imaginative leap, these may be seen as credible arboreal forms.

A bonsai, of necessity, has to be an over-simplified image. A fully-grown pine tree could have around 50 branches, but on a bonsai there is obviously not enough room. Leaves or needles will be reduced in size, though they are never so small as to be in perfect proportion to the tree. In order to accommodate such subtle simplification, bonsai has its own set of aesthetic 'rules'. These have only been developed as guides to design, they are not meant to be rigidly followed at the expense of your own artistic sense.

OPPOSITE *An impressive specimen of a bonsai tree in the Sabamiki (or Driftwood) Style. This small but sturdy Rocky Mountain Juniper* (Juniperus scopulorum) *was collected in Wyoming, USA, and is believed to be well over 300 years old.*

▶ PROPORTION ◀

In a full-sized tree the relation between the thickness of the trunk and the tree's height could be 1:30 or 1:40, perhaps more. However, in a bonsai these proportions would make the trunk appear unbelievably feeble. A proportion of 1:10 is the maximum allowable in most cases. Nowadays, the trend is toward an even tighter proportion of 1:4, or even less. A heavy trunk not only carries the implication of great age but permits the formation of interestingly textured, mature bark.

The proportional relationship between the space below the lowest branch and the total height of the tree is also important. The lowest branch should be between a quarter and one-third of the total height. A notable exception to this principle is the Literati Style, which depicts a lone conifer on a mountainside,

battling on bravely after all its neighbours have succumbed to the elements.

The proportion of the foliage will always be subject to compromise, because, although it will become smaller with trimming, it will always seem oversized. A heavy trunk will appear to balance the foliage, but choice of species is the key. Types with naturally large leaves should either be avoided or grown as larger bonsai. Only species with tiny leaves can be grown as small bonsai.

Miniature bonsai, called mame (miniature) or shohin (small), are small enough to fit into the palm of your hand. They are mostly created from species with naturally tiny leaves. In cases where larger-leaved species are used, a leaf stalk represents a branch and a single leaf, a mass of foliage.

ABOVE *This is a good example of handsome* nebari *or exposed thick roots. The roots extend outwards from a tapering trunk and are seen to anchor the tree firmly.*

The trunk

Starting at the base, the trunk should flare into surface roots (nebari) which grip the soil. The trunk should taper evenly as it progresses upward, whether straight or curved, upright, inclined or cascading, but always tapered.

If a trunk has curve at the base, it must curve throughout its length. If it is straight at the base, then it should continue straight. Curved sections alternating with straight ones look awkward.

ABOVE *These trees resemble a template for bonsai in the Group Style: demonstrating subgroups, variations in trunk girth and depth of perspective.*
TOP *The simplified image of a group of bonsai trees echoes the appearance of the copse of full-sized trees depicted above. In the spirit of the Group Planting Style, the grower has aimed for an effect that looks entirely natural.*

The branches

Trees are three-dimensional. This sounds obvious, but a mistake novices often make is to arrange the branches so that the bonsai tree looks reasonable from a particular viewing side, but does not have enough branches for symmetry to the front or the rear.

○ The first branch may be either on the left or the right but should come slightly forward.
○ The second branch should be on the opposite side, also coming slightly forward.
○ The third branch should be to the rear, to add a dimension of depth to the composition as a whole.

This pattern is followed right up the trunk, with front branches being introduced at about two-thirds of the trunk height, or higher. Keeping the lower part free of forward-growing branches keeps the trunk within view. If the trunk is lost the bonsai will look more like a shrub than a tree.

Having learned the basic rules and started to apply them, you'll see that it is practically impossible to satisfy them all unless you start with a seedling. However, do try to stick as closely as possible to the ideal.

However these rules are not set in stone; they are guidelines which should lead you to the creation of a near-perfect tree.

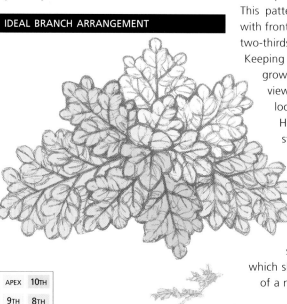

APEX	10TH
9TH	8TH
7TH	6TH
5TH	4TH
3RD	2ND
1ST	

There are several methods by which you can achieve the same result by using a little imagination and ingenuity. Don't ever think you should sacrifice your creative sensibilities for the sake of adherence to a set of arbitrary rules.

ABOVE *A pleasing branch arrangement as shown from the canopy (top) and from the front (above) of a bonsai tree. Each branch has its own space and none overshadows another.*

The rules that govern branches

- The lowest branches should be the thickest, becoming progressively thinner as they proceed up the length of the trunk.
- Branches should be more widely spaced at the bottom of the tree and should grow closer and closer together towards the top.
- On a curved trunk, branches should always emerge from the outer edge of the curve, never from the inside of the curve.
- No two branches should emerge directly opposite each other. This creates an undesirable 'handlebar' effect which immediately stops the eye from travelling up the trunk.
- Branches should always harmonize with trunks. Straight trunks must have straight branches, curved trunks, curved branches.

ABOVE LEFT *Tiny leaves and small red fruit make Cotoneaster* (Cotoneaster horizontalis*) ideal for the little shohin or mame styles.*
ABOVE RIGHT *An attractive bonsai Common Privet* (Ligustrum lucidum) *which demonstrates an excellent branch arrangement in the Upright Style.*

▸ BONSAI STYLES ◂

There are six classical bonsai styles and a growing list of nonclassical styles, as bonsai art involves new cultures and new species. Classical styles are rigidly defined and are based on an aspect of the trunk.

Nonclassical styles are governed by the overall shape, number of trunks, method of planting or another aspect of the tree. These are more loosely defined.

CLASSICAL STYLES

Formal Upright (*Chokkan*)
A straight, upright trunk that carries on all the way to the very top of the tree and has a uniform taper from the base to the apex. This style is most appropriately used for, and associated with, bonsai conifers.

Slanting (*Shakan*)
This is a variation on the formal and informal upright styles. The trunk (naturally enough), is inclined either to the left or right. Conifers or broadleaved species can be treated this way.

Informal Upright (*Moyogi*)
This is the most common bonsai style. The trunk describes a series of curves beginning at the base and continuing up to the apex, while maintaining the uniform taper usually used for conifers or broadleaved trees.

Broom (*Hokidachi*)
The most authentically tree-like of all bonsai styles. The trunk is straight and the branches fan out, forking to form a symmetrical, domed canopy. This style is best confined to broadleaved species.

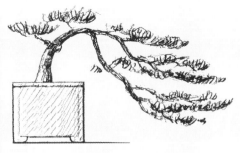

Cascade (*Kengai*)

Inspired by the image of a tree clinging to a cliff face. In this style, the lowest point of the tree must fall below the base of the pot. Both cascade and semi-cascade styles should be planted in pots that are deeper than they are wide. Best for conifers, as broadleaved species may be weakened at their lowest point.

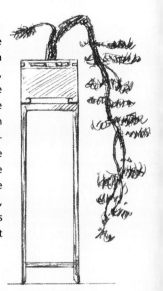

Semi-cascade (*Han-kengai*)

This style mimics a tree clinging to a mountain ledge, where its lowest branch cascades to below the rim of the pot. It is most commonly used for conifers, and sometimes for broadleaved species.

NONCLASSICAL STYLES

Windswept (*Fukinagashi*)

The name says it all. This is probably the most difficult style to create successfully. The tree must look as if it lives on a wind-blasted, exposed hillside and not as if it is just falling over. The Windswept style may be used for any species.

Literati (*Bunjingi*)

Named after a group of Chinese scholars who established it, this style involves a single conifer with a slender trunk and minimal foliage. It represents a tree that once stood on the edge of a forest but is now the only one left standing. Appropriate for conifers; usually pines.

Exposed Root (*Neagari*)

Similar to root-over-rock, but without a rock. This dramatic style is rare, as it is difficult to create and, consequently, is highly prized.

Spiral Trunk (*Bankan*)

An unnatural style that involves an artificially spiralled or twisted trunk. Once common in China, it is now almost extinct. Any species can be ruined by having this style applied to it!

Driftwood (*Sharimiki, Sabamiki*)

An abstract style, based on mountain trees that have had areas of bark stripped away by the elements or by disease. Driftwood areas, (*shari*) bleached with lime sulphur, mimic sun-damage and contrast nicely with the foliage. Conifers are suitable species.

Planted-in-rock (*Ishitsuki*)

This is like a miniature landscape. A large rock has cavities, natural or man-made, into which the trees are planted. The trees are shaped according to their relative positions on the mock mountain. For reasons of scale, this style works well with conifers.

Root-over-rock (*Sekijôju*)

Imitates a tree growing on the rocky bank of a stream, where passing flood waters have eroded the soil and exposed roots that are tightly clasped to the rock. Broadleaved or coniferous species with sturdy, thick roots are best.

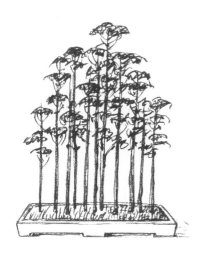

Double-trunk (*Sôju*)

This paired-trunk style involves a larger and a smaller trunk joined at the base. If the trunks are separated, the style becomes known as the 'mother and child'. The Japanese term remains the same for both paired-trunk styles.

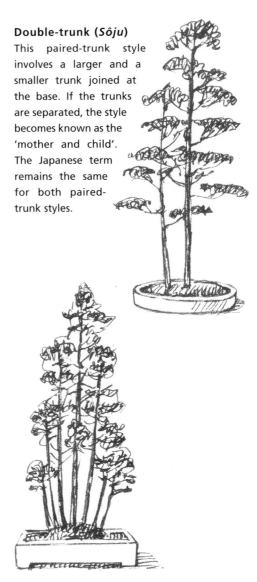

Forest (*Yose-ue*)

Any number of trees can be used, provided they have sympathetic lines and different trunk thicknesses. Uneven numbers work best up to around a dozen – after which it does not matter much. Species with small leaves give the best results.

Raft (*Netsunagari, Ikadabuki*)

Fallen trees may survive by thrusting new roots into the soil from the trunk. Former branches grow upwards to form new trunks. This form should follow the criteria for forest styles. Broadleaved trees or conifers can be utilized.

Clump (*Kabudachi*)

This imitates the natural phenomenon which sometimes occurs when a tree dies, or is felled. New stems shoot up from the stump and, in time, grow together at the base. Broadleaved trees are used because not many conifers will re-grow from old stumps.

▶ DISPLAY ◀

Bonsai trees spend most of their time on growing benches in the garden, or in a suitable position inside the house. However, occasionally they are displayed in order to provide a focal point in a room, such as when an important guest is expected.

Serious collectors with many established bonsai choose always to have at least one tree on show. But no tree should be displayed indoors for more than a few days at a time, because the conditions will be less than perfect for its health.

In fact, if a deciduous tree is brought into a warm house in winter, it may start to break dormancy before it goes out into the cold again. This always retards the tree's spring growth and may prove fatal.

In Japan, bonsai are usually displayed in a custom-made alcove called a tokonoma. This is a low platform covered with plain matting and flanked by enclosing walls. Traditionally, one side has a window-like opening, edged with natural wood. The tree is always placed just off centre on a stand or table, never directly on the platform. According to custom, two other elements are included in the display: a scroll on the wall behind it, depicting some calligraphy, or a sympathetic scene from nature; and an accent item, which may be a viewing stone (*suiseki*), a plant (such as an alpine grass) or a second, smaller bonsai.

At home there is no need for you to go to such lengths to display your bonsai in the dignified manner considered appropriate in

ABOVE *A bonsai tree displayed in a Japanese tokonoma, or alcove, is complemented by the juxtaposition of an ancient scroll and an accent piece which may be a* suiseki *(viewing stone) or other harmonious object. The composition achieves its aim by fostering a sense of serenity in the viewer.*

the East. The important thing is that you keep the display simple. The only essential is a backdrop, consisting of a blank wall with a plain level surface in front of it.

It is practical to have a raised surface on which to stand the tree, if only to protect your furniture. A small table or a mat made of split bamboo looks appropriate and attractive. A friend of mine has used an inverted plain wooden tea-tray to great effect.

You may dispense with the scroll, but an accent of some kind enlivens the display. Make sure that your choice of feature is in harmony with the bonsai. A rugged, weather-beaten style of bonsai might be accented by a cool, smooth viewing stone, representing a mountain, or by a small alpine plant. A colourful lowland maple would be enhanced by a pot of wild or meadow grasses.

If your trees live out of doors, bring them in for only a few days at a time. Any longer, and they will sulk when put back out again.

Displaying bonsai

When you display bonsai trees, follow these guidelines to ensure they are in pristine condition:

- Clean the containers thoroughly (don't overlook their feet!). Unglazed pots can be burnished using a little vegetable oil and a lint-free cloth.
- Clear any debris from the soil and plant new moss if the old is not in mint condition.
- Remove training wires that are no longer in use. Any wire that must remain in place should be as unobtrusive as possible.
- Clean the bark on both the trunk and branches with a toothbrush and water.
- Trim the tree carefully. In summer, trees should be trimmed a week or two before they are displayed, so that new leaves can emerge to freshen up the colours, and the plant looks at its best.
- Snip off dead or discoloured foliage, as well as any faded or overblown flowers.

TOP *A sensitive display of a flowering bonsai that does not look out of place in a contemporary Western home.*

Your Own Bonsai
COLLECTION
Where and how to begin

Bonsai is a time-consuming and compelling hobby. Once you're hooked, it becomes a way of life. The initial challenge of keeping your trees in shape and in good health gives way to the thrill of developing them further.

▸ READY-MADE OR HOMEGROWN? ◂

Bonsai enthusiasts fall into two main categories, those who collect established trees and those who grow their own. Both these approaches are able to offer their practitioners unique experiences which are deeply satisfying.

Growing your own
Growing your own bonsai need not start by being expensive. Plants are free if grown from seed or cuttings and, for the first few years, any old pot will serve as a container. Even if you choose to buy nursery plants to work with, they will still be relatively cheap compared with ready-grown bonsai of whatever quality. Depending on your ultimate aim, growing your own bonsai can be great fun, and the rewards to be had in terms of appreciation of the final result – plus the knowledge that it has been achieved by your own hand – is a joy beyond compare!

Almost all bonsai enthusiasts attempt to grow their own trees at some point, but most begin their lifelong love affair with bonsai by buying a tree. You will find all you need to know about growing your own bonsai in this book, starting on p119.

OPPOSITE *Bursting into fresh spring foliage, this is a bonsai larch (Larix spp.) in the Literati or Bunjin Style. The style, named after a group of scholars literate in the arts, mimics the restrained elegance of calligraphy in its flowing trunk line.*

Buying ready-made bonsai

Bonsai always appear to be expensive for what you get. In saying this, I don't mean to suggest that retailers make vast profits. Far from it; no-one gets rich selling bonsai. When you consider that even the cheapest supermarket bonsai has had some care lavished on it, at least some pruning of branches and roots, and that it has then been transported half-way round the world, a price that is equivalent to that of a cinema outing for two does not seem unreasonable.

When it comes to larger, more established bonsai, the price may be on a par with that of a second-hand car. But just think what you're getting. The tree may be anything from 20 to 100 years old, perhaps more. It would initially have been pruned and the main branches would have been wired into position. Then the tree would probably have spent up to 25 years in a growing field, before being potted up into a training box. During its spell in the ground it would have to have been lifted every few years to have its roots cut back, the branches pruned and shaped and the wires removed. All highly skilled, time-consuming jobs.

Once in the training box, the grower is likely to have sold the tree on to a refining nursery. Here, experts would have attended to its every need. They would check on its development, visiting it often in the growing season to trim, prune and shape the branches. Every year or two, it would have been repotted, at which time the roots would need to have received the same attention as the branches. After several years in the refining nursery, it would finally have been potted into an appropriate bonsai container. Then, and only then, would it have been offered for sale!

If it were to be sold for export, the bonsai would have been removed from its pot (which would have to be shipped separately) and carefully wired into a custom-built crate, with the roots packed in moist sphagnum moss. The packing crate, with others, would then have been shipped in a temperature-controlled hold to its new destination. Before it could be put on display and sold, it would have been inspected by officials to make sure it was free of pests and disease and, even then, would have had to spend up to six months in quarantine. Little wonder that the best-quality bonsai are quite expensive!

As you can see, there is every reason for quality bonsai trees, which have enjoyed many years of care from dedicated specialists, to be regarded as living things of great intrinsic worth. Get the best tree you can afford and treat as you would a faithful friend.

ABOVE *Ugly little plants like this are all too often sold as bonsai trees, yet this one resembles neither an ideal tree, nor an ideal bonsai!*

Buyer's guide

When buying a bonsai, bear in mind that it is important to find a dealer whose advice you can trust. These miniature plants are living entities and, due to the amount of care that goes into producing them, good ones are not cheap. A tree that is able to thrive in the conditions you can provide for it will reward you with many years of pleasure.

TOP *This Chinese Juniper (*Junipernus chinensis *var.* sargentii) *has an interesting trunk and attractive branch placement. However, its foliage has been neglected and it has too many branches. Careful improvements will reveal its intrinsic beauty.*

ABOVE *After some dedicated effort, the new, improved bonsai shines through. Deadwood areas contrast nicely with the glossy foliage. Branches and shoots have been wired to create a crisp outline. The foliage has space to spread out and there is plenty of room for fresh growth.*

Indoor bonsai

These days, in most Western countries, small and rather tired bonsai are sold in all sorts of odd places, from supermarkets to home-care stores, and even on petrol station forecourts. I have seen tropical bonsai incongruously being offered for sale from market stalls in the dead of winter. The poor things were moribund even before they were sold.

In one sense, the proliferation of cheap, so-called bonsai has introduced the pastime to a wider audience, bringing the many joys of the hobby to people who have later become dedicated enthusiasts. But in the vast majority of instances these small trees quickly succumb, not because their new owners have mistreated them, but simply because they are unable to bear the succession of shocks to which they have been exposed. The care instructions (if any), which come with them, are invariably inadequate and the sales staff quite unable to offer any useful advice.

You may say, 'Well, I bought a bonsai from a supermarket and it's still alive'. Good; you're exceptionally lucky! My advice, though, is that next time round, you seek out a specialized bonsai supplier or a general nursery which deals in bonsai. At least there, the staff will have some knowledge of plant species and their care. And you'll get a real live bonsai tree, rather than a sad little basket-case!

A good indicator of whether or not a store is a reliable supplier of bonsai is the range of related products and equipment they sell. If the outlet also stocks the appropriate books, tools, wire and pots, you may be assured that they take bonsai seriously and have other satisfied customers.

ABOVE *Specialist indoor bonsai nurseries stock healthy trees and are able to offer sound advice to buyers. They also carry tools, fertilizers, containers, and books on bonsai.*

Outdoor bonsai

Most trees dislike sudden changes in their environment; for example, even normally hardy trees will deteriorate rapidly if kept indoors for more than a few days. It naturally follows, therefore that if you want to start off by growing trees outdoors, where they belong, you should buy them from a supplier who is as committed to the art of bonsai as you are. Do not ever buy outdoor trees from a store that keeps them inside.

If possible, seek out a nursery or garden centre which specializes in bonsai, even if you have to go some distance to get to one. The trip will be well worth your time and trouble. There, you will discover a wide selection of species and a knowledgeable staff who will be delighted to offer you the benefit of their wide experience. You'll also be able to get all the proper tools and equipment you will need in order to begin your hobby. Furthermore, many good bonsai nurseries offer holiday care services, training courses, workshops and, often, potting and trimming services. They will also be able to help you nurse your tree back to health if it takes ill.

TOP *The best nurseries ensure that their outdoor stock is in prime condition. Buying from a professional supplier minimizes the shock to the tree on relocation.*

▸ WHICH SPECIES TO BUY ◂

Before you decide whether you would prefer a maple or a pine, a juniper or carmona, first give careful consideration to where you intend to keep your bonsai.

- ○ Will you keep your bonsai indoors or out?
- ○ If it is indoors, are you able to offer it sufficient light?
- ○ Is the atmosphere in your home dry, or can you provide your plants with the optimum humidity level they require?
- ○ If a tree is to be kept outside, will it be in full sun all day or can it be offered some shade?
- ○ How cold does the winter get in your area? Some species demand winter cold for their survival.
- ○ Do you have a shed or garage to shelter delicate trees during spells of bitter cold?

The checklist might seem daunting, but don't worry; a full list of cultivation requirements for the most popular species of bonsai appears among the species profiles in the Directory (see p161). Besides, the basic formula is straightforward.

So-called 'indoor' bonsai are tropical or subtropical species that will not withstand severe cold, but can tolerate the conditions in most homes. Some prefer more humidity, but all will survive in a reasonably mild atmosphere. Most of these species will live very happily outside in the tropical, and sometimes even the subtropical, parts of the world.

Hardy trees require winter dormancy and won't tolerate the conditions indoors at any time. Hardy species can't be grown effectively in subtropical or tropical regions.

Generally, reputable bonsai retailers in tropical countries won't sell hardy trees, nor will salespeople in cold countries sell tropical

This list demonstrates the difficulty rating of the most popular indoor tropical and subtropical species, being easy and the most demanding.

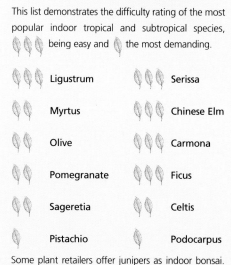

Some plant retailers offer junipers as indoor bonsai. Don't take this seriously, as no self-respecting juniper would survive for long indoors.

TOP *A really well-ramified bonsai elm (Ulmus spp.), displaying a neat branch layout that is able to make a strong statement, even in the winter months, when it has lost its leaves.*

species, unless they are specifically intended for indoor cultivation in ideal surroundings. Approaching a reliable dealer makes your choice that much easier.

It's an idea to subtly question the sales staff before parting with your money. Ask them questions to which you know the answers, such as: 'Is Serissa hardy?' or 'Can you keep pines indoors?' If the reply to either question is 'yes', walk away!

Spoiled for choice?

For first-time buyers, the choice should be between species that are easy to cultivate and those that are not. By far the most resilient species are varieties of fig (*Ficus* spp.), closely followed by Chinese Elm (*Ulmus parvifolia*), which is also sometimes called *Zelkova sinica*, and Serissa (*Serissa foetida*), all of which will tolerate a broad range of conditions.

Hardy trees are easy to cultivate if given the right soil and growing conditions. Conifers generally prefer a lot of sun, while deciduous species prefer shade in the afternoon, or semi-shade all day. Pines can be left outdoors in very cold weather (if out of the wind), whereas maples and elms require the protection of a shed or garage in cold weather.

Bearing in mind all of the above, the final decision depends on your taste. Do you prefer the visual strength and stability of a pine or a juniper, or the delicacy and seasonal changes you may expect from a Japanese Maple? Perhaps the spring flowers of an azalea or a crab apple are appealing to you, or you may prefer the fine twigs of elm or cotoneaster.

Having made up your mind as to your preference of species, you get to choose the actual tree. Follow the tips given in the box on the opposite page, and enjoy the experience.

TOP *Juvenile juniper foliage, green and glossy with good health.*
CENTRE *An example of an attractive flare at the base of the trunk.*
BOTTOM *This foliage is giving early warning signs of disease or infestation.*

▶ WHAT TO LOOK FOR IN A TREE ◀

No matter what species of tree you decide upon, or where you choose to buy it, there are some points that are worth checking out:

○ Trees offered for sale should be labelled with their botanical (Latin) names, so that you can be certain of the type you are buying.

○ Ensure the tree you fancy is well-rooted. Rock it gently; if it moves easily in the pot, there are problems with the roots, so choose another specimen.

○ Check the base of the pot for adequate drainage holes.

○ Check the tips of new shoots for abnormal growth, which is often indicative of either overfeeding or of aphid infestation.

○ Foliage should be glossy and of a healthy colour. Dry or yellow leaves are warning signs of disease. Examine the foliage sprouting from short inner shoots, as these will be needed to maintain the tree's shape.

○ Clusters of dead twigs may indicate insect attack or may merely be due to an accidentally broken branch. Worse, they might also be a sign of a more serious internal, or even root, problems.

○ If the tree has training wires on its branches, make sure they haven't begun to cut into the bark, as any scars will take many years to heal, if indeed they ever do.

○ Examine both the trunk and branches for old wiring scars (avoid damaged trees).

○ Finally, unless you are experienced, always buy your bonsai during spring and summer, when they are in full leaf.

○ Choose a tree that is both healthy and well-shaped, and has potential for future development. Bear in mind that as you gain experience and skills, your own aesthetic judgement will become more refined.

Surface roots (nebari)

The nebari, or visible surface roots, are most important when selecting a bonsai. The base of the trunk should flare out, and the roots should radiate evenly all around the trunk, in order to get a firm grip on the soil. High roots, roots that cross over each other, or ones that are oddly formed should be avoided, because they are never going to look attractive.

Some bonsai suppliers glue pebbles to the soil surface for decorative purposes. This is not only a ridiculous practice, but the stones will impede water penetration and, eventually, this is bound to cause the death of the tree.

Trunk

Look for a trunk with an even taper from base to apex. Heavy pruning scars can take decades to heal, so unless they can be incorporated as a design feature, they are best avoided.

Branches

Branches should be distributed all around the trunk, but with none on the lower two-thirds in the front. No two branches should emerge at the same level on the trunk. The lowest branches should be the thickest. Look out for ugly swellings where branches join the trunk. Avoid trees whose branches have long, straight sections without forks.

Foliage

The leaves should be in good condition, glossy and without any signs of disease or dryness. Ideally, the leaves should not be so large as to make the rest of the miniature tree appear out of proportion.

Overall style

This is where your personal taste comes in. Remember that pines should be shaped like real pine trees and maples should look like maples. Don't be persuaded to buy a tree with a bizarre, contorted trunk or tangled roots, because when you begin to take the hobby seriously, you may regret it.

Whether you plump for a ready-made bonsai or choose to grow your own from scratch, you should learn the correct techniques for shaping, repotting and, most importantly, the best way to keep your bonsai in peak condition.

ABOVE LEFT *Pruning cuts should be sealed immediately with Japanese cut paste. This is a putty-like compound that keeps the cut edge moist, thus preventing excessive contraction of the surrounding tissue.*

ABOVE RIGHT *Check for wires that are becoming so tight that the bark is beginning to bulge ominously. The advice comes too late for this unfortunate tree, as the wounds it has suffered will cause permanent scarring.*

OPPOSITE TOP *Unsightly nebari cannot be hidden. Surface roots are a feature of bonsai, so good ones greatly enhance a tree's appearance.*

OPPOSITE BOTTOM *The surface roots on this bonsai, which is in the process of being repotted, spread attractively from the base of the trunk.*

Keeping Your Bonsai
Alive
Caring for your bonsai

Caring for bonsai is largely a matter of common sense, as all plants, regardless of size, have the same basic requirements. If these are met, your plant will spontaneously demonstrate its gratitude by thriving.

▶ **WATERING** ◀

A bonsai might easily die if it were to go without water for more than a day in high summer. This may make keeping a tree sound like a major commitment; however, it soon becomes as much part of your routine as brushing your teeth. Getting the watering schedule just right usually takes a little practice, but it will fall into place. Once you have repotted the tree into your own choice of soil mixture (see p110), it will become a great deal easier.

In spite of the bonsai's dependence on regular watering, it is a fact that more trees are killed by drowning than by drought.

Too much water standing for too long will starve the roots of oxygen, after which they will die and begin to rot. By the time you notice that all is not well, it may be too late. Even if it isn't too late, your first reaction might well be to give the plant some more water – just in case!

It's impossible to mention this basic rule too often: never give a bonsai a drink if it doesn't need watering.

When to water

The main problem with watering newly acquired trees is guessing how damp the soil may be below the surface, which might give the appearance of being quite dry. When you use a mix of coarse, open soil you'll be able to scratch away the surface particles in a corner of the pot to see just how moist it is underneath. Many Far Eastern bonsai producers use clay-based soils which can become heavily compacted after a year or so, making this estimation that much more difficult to make.

However, there is an easy way to tell how much moisture is in the soil deep down in the pot.

OPPOSITE *Water plants gently but thoroughly from above, with a very fine rose on the watering can. Wait a few minutes and repeat the process.*

THE CHOPSTICK TEST

Take a softwood chopstick (a kebab stick will do), and push it right into the soil, all the way to the very bottom of the container. If you feel your probe hitting a root, try another part of the pot; corners are best. Leave it in place for 20 minutes or so, then remove it and feel the end that was buried in the soil. If it feels moist, there's no need to water just yet. If it's on the dry side, you should water, and if it feels bone dry, you should have watered the tree already! Once you have watered the plant, replace the stick and you won't have to wait 20 minutes the next time.

Try not to get into the habit of watering at the same time every day, regardless of the weather and the season. Rather, use the stick to check every day for the first year or so, until you get the hang of it. You'll be surprised how much your bonsai's water requirements will change as the weeks pass.

1 TO TEST THE MOISTURE CONTENT OF THE SOIL, INSERT A SOFTWOOD STICK DEEP INTO THE POT.

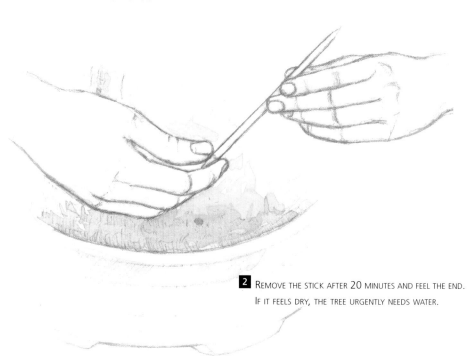

2 REMOVE THE STICK AFTER 20 MINUTES AND FEEL THE END. IF IT FEELS DRY, THE TREE URGENTLY NEEDS WATER.

How to water

Bonsai are best watered from above, using the fine rose on a watering can. If you don't use a rose it's impossible to soak the soil evenly. The water is likely to run across the surface and down between the soil and the side of the pot. Add water gently until it begins to flow out of the drainage holes. Wait a few minutes and repeat. That's all! The pot should feel noticeably heavier after watering. If it doesn't, the soil may not be absorbing water properly for one reason or another, so change to the immersion technique described overleaf.

Keep a spray bottle to hand and give the trees a misting every so often. This is especially important for trees kept indoors, where the atmosphere is usually dry. Spray the undersides of the leaves as well as the tops, but try not to drench the soil at the same time.

What sort of water

In general, water fit for humans is fit for plants. Nothing added to tap water can harm plants in any way. However, some plants don't tolerate lime (these plants are called calcifuges). So, if a bonsai falls into this category, and the water in your area is hard, use only stored rainwater. When this is not available, bottled water is the only option. Beware of domestic water softeners; they work by replacing calcium in the water with sodium, which is harmful to trees.

The only harm hard water may do to non-calcifuge trees is a slight encrustation of lime on the exposed roots. These whitish deposits can easily be removed with rainwater and an old toothbrush.

TOP *Bonsai trees in the serene environs of the Yuyuan garden in Shanghai, China, enjoy the soft, soaking rain. Nature's method of watering is ideal: the soil is thoroughly saturated, the foliage is sprayed and welcome humidity is provided.*

Immersing the pot

Some of the care leaflets provided by retailers recommend immersing the pot in a bowl of water for several minutes. This method is, at best, an emergency treatment, necessary only when the soil has dried out so much that it repels water, or when the clay-based soils commonly used in the Far East have become compacted. In such cases, the surface may appear damp, giving the impression that the soil has been thoroughly soaked when in fact the water has just run down between the earth and the pot and out of the drainage holes. If you do have to immerse the pot, use

water which is at room temperature, and lower the pot slowly into it, until the water just covers the soil. At this point air bubbles will begin rising from the soil. Once all the the air bubbles have stopped, the soil should be wet through. When you remove the pot from the water, it should feel much heavier; if it doesn't, then it is not damp throughout.

Resorting to the immersion of the container in water on a regular basis, does have its drawbacks. If the soil contains a large amount of clay, the particles will start to disintegrate and eventually will amalgamate into a solid mass. New trees should be repotted into a container of good, friable soil before this becomes a problem. It is not a good idea to leave the plant struggling in sodden clay until the roots become water-logged and begin to rot. By the time this becomes obvious, the health of the plant will have been compromised.

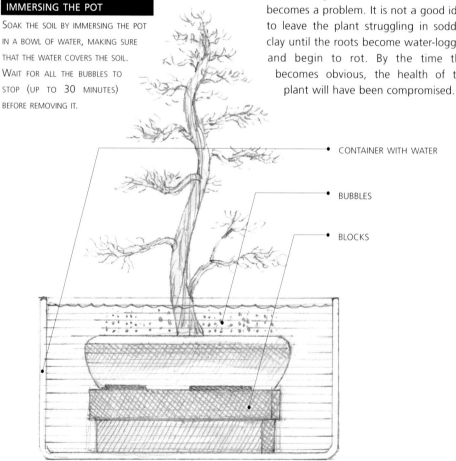

IMMERSING THE POT

SOAK THE SOIL BY IMMERSING THE POT IN A BOWL OF WATER, MAKING SURE THAT THE WATER COVERS THE SOIL. WAIT FOR ALL THE BUBBLES TO STOP (UP TO 30 MINUTES) BEFORE REMOVING IT.

CONTAINER WITH WATER

BUBBLES

BLOCKS

We all like to take holidays now and then. Those of us for whom bonsai has become a way of life prefer to go away in the winter months, which for many people may not be practical. So, how can you make sure your bonsai trees get properly watered while you are enjoying a break?

Holiday care services
Most good specialist bonsai nurseries will care for trees while their owners are away from home. Some charge a small fee, but many offer this as a free service to their customers. At a nursery, you can be sure that professional horticulturalists will take excellent care of your precious trees.

Friends or neighbours
Most people ask a neighbour to water their bonsai. If you do this, invite your victim to watch you water a few times. Demonstrate the stick test and remember that most kindly neighbours over-water, just to be on the safe side. While a week's saturation shouldn't do too much harm, two weeks could be fatal. Don't forget to mention regular misting!

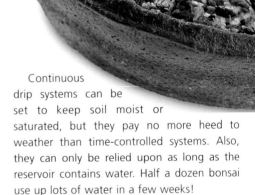

Automatic systems
A variety of automatic watering systems are available to home gardeners. Time-controlled systems can be set to water at predetermined intervals. They sound ideal but there are snags. One is that they take no account of the weather and will water even in the rain! They also water from above, which means that the foliage may get soaked, leaving the soil dry.

Continuous drip systems can be set to keep soil moist or saturated, but they pay no more heed to weather than time-controlled systems. Also, they can only be relied upon as long as the reservoir contains water. Half a dozen bonsai use up lots of water in a few weeks!

Soil sensors are reliable and will prompt a pump to supply water when the soil reaches a specific degree of dryness. Use one if you can afford it. If you decide to use an automatic watering system, be sure to have it installed about a month before you go away, so you'll have plenty of time to test and adjust it.

ABOVE *If the soil has become compacted, or even if it is bone dry, it may well repel water from above and the roots will suffer from dehydration.*
TOP *A tree being killed by kindness! A well-meaning neighbour has saturated the bonsai pot in the owner's absence. Water pooling permanently on the surface of the soil means that the roots are drowning in standing water, and will rot.*

1 TAKE A STRIP OF CAPILLARY MATTING, OR A PIECE OF OLD TOWELLING TWISTED INTO A 'ROPE'. CAREFULLY EASE THE TREE FROM ITS POT AND THREAD THE WICK THROUGH A DRAINAGE HOLE. LEAVE SOME INSIDE, COILED ROUND THE BASE OF THE POT, AND ENOUGH OUTSIDE TO REACH A RESERVOIR OF WATER. THEN REPLACE THE TREE IN THE POT.

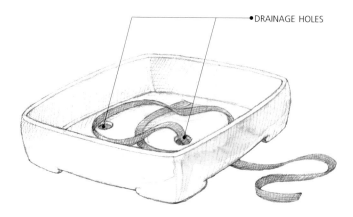

•DRAINAGE HOLES

2 PUT A RESERVOIR OF WATER NEARBY AND DRAPE THE END OF THE WICK IN IT. THE CLOSER THE RESERVOIR IS TO THE POT, THE BETTER THIS WORKS. IF YOU WISH, YOU CAN USE ANOTHER WICK LAID ACROSS THE SURFACE OF THE SOIL, AS WELL.

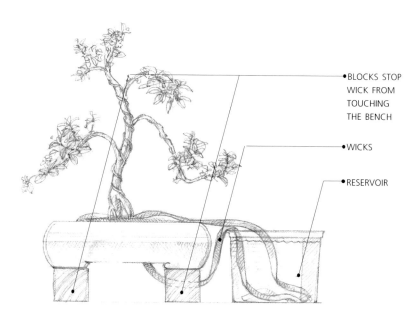

•BLOCKS STOP WICK FROM TOUCHING THE BENCH

•WICKS

•RESERVOIR

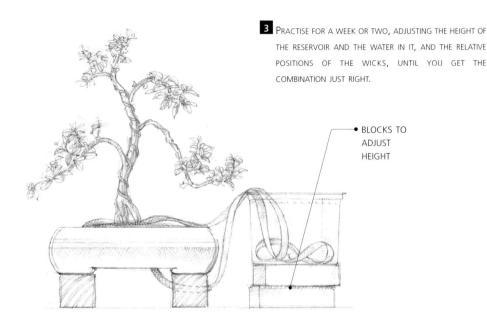

3 PRACTISE FOR A WEEK OR TWO, ADJUSTING THE HEIGHT OF THE RESERVOIR AND THE WATER IN IT, AND THE RELATIVE POSITIONS OF THE WICKS, UNTIL YOU GET THE COMBINATION JUST RIGHT.

BLOCKS TO
ADJUST
HEIGHT

Short breaks

If you're only going to be away for a few days, the best way to reduce your bonsai's water requirements is by putting it in a cool, shady place, where it will be surrounded by other green plants. The combination of the shade that the other plants afford your bonsai trees, and the additional humidity that is provided by the surrounding foliage, is able to reduce a plant's water uptake by 50 per cent or perhaps even more.

To be sure your trees get enough moisture, it is an idea to bury the pots in moist peat or sand, after the plant has been given a thorough watering. Settle the pot in to ensure that the peat or sand makes close contact with the unglazed base of the bonsai pot. Then erect a plastic 'tent', supported by wires, over the tree, making certain that no part of the plastic comes into contact with the leaves. This simple arrangement should keep the bonsai tree well-watered and in good health for three or four days, or perhaps even longer.

RIGHT *Burying the pots in moist peat or sand helps to keep them cool, creates local atmospheric humidity and allows some of the moisture to permeate upwards through the drainage holes.*

▶ LIGHT ◀

Green plants need light in order to survive. Without light, the leaves are not able to photosynthesize the sugars that provide the plant with vital energy. However, there is an important difference between light and sun.

OUTDOOR SUNLIGHT

TALL TREES PROVIDE IDEAL SHADE. DECIDUOUS SPECIES, ESPECIALLY, ALLOW PLENTY OF SUN TO FILTER THROUGH IN WINTER. NEVER PUT BONSAI DIRECTLY BELOW THE BRANCHES OF OTHER TREES, AS TANNINS (WHICH HARM THE BONSAI TREES) MAY BE LEACHED FROM THEM. FALLING INSECTS AND BIRD-DROPPINGS ARE ALSO OVERHEAD HAZARDS. IT IS ESSENTIAL THAT THE MOST TENDER BONSAI TREES BE SHADED FROM THE EXTREME HEAT OF THE AFTERNOON SUN.

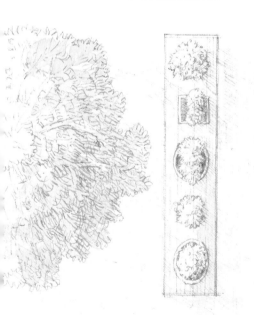

Direct sunlight contains ultraviolet radiation which, at high levels, can be harmful to some plants. The heat of mid-summer sunshine in combination with UV radiation could cause considerable damage to your bonsai tree. Just imagine how you would feel if you were exposed to the heat of the sun all day, every day. To compound the problem, the roots of small bonsai trees are not buried deep in the cool earth, but compressed into containers. The pots heat up quickly in the sun and it is not unusual for them to reach temperatures well in excess of 40°C (over 100°F).

Almost all gardens have some patches that get full sun and others that get hardly any sun at all. What you must do is to choose the best position for your tree. Overhead light is important, because it's 'pure' light. Shading a tree from above with, for example, coloured plastic, deprives it of much of the beneficial radiation as well as blocking the harmful rays.

If you do need to provide overhead shade, use netting or shade cloth, preferably in white, which will block out a proportion of direct sunlight (depending on the shade rating of the

RIGHT *Shade netting allows light to filter gently through to the trees but protects vulnerable ones from the more harmful ultraviolet rays of the sun.*

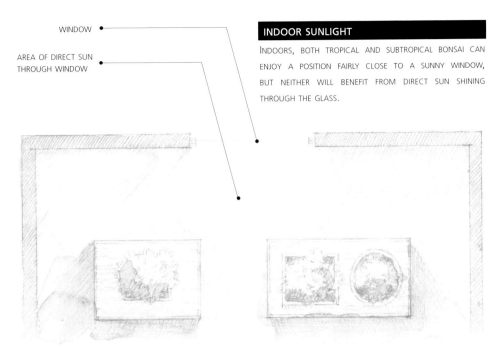

WINDOW •

AREA OF DIRECT SUN
THROUGH WINDOW •

INDOORS, BOTH TROPICAL AND SUBTROPICAL BONSAI CAN ENJOY A POSITION FAIRLY CLOSE TO A SUNNY WINDOW, BUT NEITHER WILL BENEFIT FROM DIRECT SUN SHINING THROUGH THE GLASS.

chosen netting), while allowing just enough ambient light to be reflected downward. The small spots of sunlight that do reach the leaves will move as the sun does, so no part of any leaf will be overexposed.

Alternatively, adjacent trees can provide excellent dappled shade for your bonsai, provided you don't place the trees directly beneath the branches. Apart from sheltering them from welcome rain, there are many insect pests which may fall on your bonsai from above; not to mention what birds might drop! As heavy rain filters through foliage and off the branches of some species of tree, it picks up tannins which retard the growth of any vegetation below, including bonsai.

Sun through glass If you keep bonsai trees indoors, don't be tempted to put them on the sunniest window ledges. As direct sunlight passes through glass, the heat is intensified, and your tree will bake. The best situation for plants growing indoors is near to a bright window but out of reach of direct rays of sunlight. Fine white shade netting helps to create optimal light conditions.

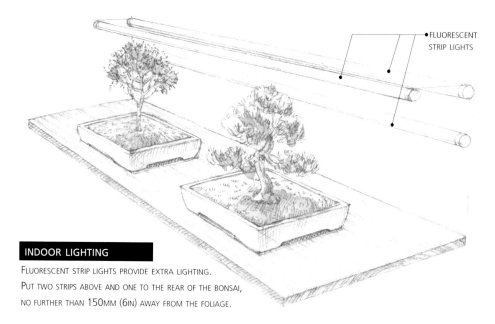

FLUORESCENT STRIP LIGHTS PROVIDE EXTRA LIGHTING. PUT TWO STRIPS ABOVE AND ONE TO THE REAR OF THE BONSAI, NO FURTHER THAN 150MM (6IN) AWAY FROM THE FOLIAGE.

Artificial light

On dull winter days, or if you don't have a well-placed window, your indoor bonsai may need supplementary lighting.

Balanced-spectrum horticultural lighting systems, which are widely available, can be expensive to buy and to run, but are perfect for the job. However, if you can't afford a fancy system, you can use plain fluorescent strip lights. Two 30-watt strips mounted above the trees, 150mm (6in) from the foliage, plus one strip behind, will be adequate. If you place them any further away than this, the light intensity is dramatically reduced. Remember to rotate your trees daily and do not leave lights on for more than 16 hours a day.

ABOVE *Plants derive the maximum benefit from filtered sunlight. These plants are being properly nurtured in good growing conditions.*

▶ TEMPERATURE ◀

Trees can be divided into hardy species which tolerate freezing, subtropical species which can withstand cold (but not freezing), and tropical species which must be kept warm at all times.

Virtually all hardy species, and many subtropical ones, require a dormant period each year. This is induced by the shortening of

TEMPERATURE RANGE

THE RANGE OF TEMPERATURES PREFERRED BY VARIOUS CATEGORIES OF PLANTS THAT MAKE GOOD BONSAI.

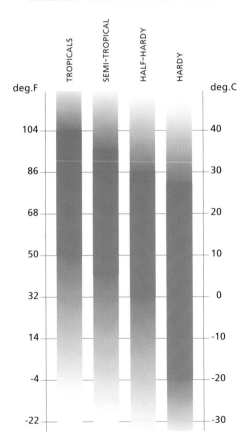

days and the drop in mean temperature. Hardy varieties may actually need a period of subzero temperatures to become dormant. Without sufficient dormancy, the trees will deteriorate, and will eventually die.

Freezing kills nonhardy trees by bursting the cells in the shoots, branches and roots. In hardy trees, the cells in both the roots and the woody parts are able to withstand freezing to some extent, but even with hardy trees, it is more important to protect the roots from freezing than to protect the tops. Two species in particular, Trident Maple (*Acer buergerianum*) and Chinese Elm (*Ulmus parvifolia*), have fleshy roots which may suffer permanent cell damage once they have been frozen hard.

Tropical and sub-tropical species tolerate high temperatures quite comfortably, provided humidity levels are adequate and the roots are not allowed to bake, but hardy trees can suffer heat stress. At temperatures above 30°C (86°F), most hardy trees shut down. The stomata remain closed to prevent transpiration, water uptake is reduced and the tree stops growing. If this condition is allowed to continue for too long, the leaves will fall and the young shoots may die. Keeping the pot cool is a good idea, while providing well-ventilated shade and spraying the foliage regularly will also help to keep the tree active.

TOP *Pieces of terracotta roofing tile may not look attractive when balanced over bonsai containers, but they help the roots to stay cool in hot weather.*

KEEPING YOUR BONSAI
HEALTHY
Fertilizers and pest control

Green plants need three essential nutrients in order to thrive: nitrogen, phosphorus and potassium. Most fertilizers contain all three in various proportions, and at a variety of concentrations. But even the healthiest plants can fall prey to insect pests and fungal diseases.

▸ FEEDING ◂

If you look at the contents listed on any fertilizer pack, you will see the initials N (for nitrogen), P (phosphorus), and K (potassium), followed by three numbers. This gives the ratio between the three nutrients, and the relative strength of the fertilizer. The higher the number, the stronger the concentration of the nutrient. For example, NPK 6:6:6 is a balanced fertilizer of moderate strength, whereas NPK 20:5:5 is a high nitrogen fertilizer, which is generally used for lawns.

The pack will list details of dilution and application rates. Following these instructions is important because, if you use less than the recommended dose, the strength diminishes.

If you use too much fertilizer, however, you could cause 'root burn', which can damage plants. It is generally better to use less than the recommended dose rather than too much. Many manufacturers advise the application of half-strength solutions more frequently, rather than infrequent applications of the full-strength mixtures .

In addition to the three basic nutrients, plants need trace elements, or macro and micro nutrients, which are essential for plant growth. Fertile soils contain small amounts of such chemicals but the inert components of most bonsai soils do not. Some organic fertilizers provide a few trace elements, like magnesium, zinc and iron, but not all the micro nutrients that plants require. On the other hand, many chemical fertilizers do contain some of these elements and, if they are present, they will be listed on the pack.

If you prefer to use organic feed, search gardening catalogues for specific additives. Keen gardeners might be tempted to use

OPPOSITE *The rationale that underlies the art of bonsai is to create objects of lasting beauty, so it makes perfect sense to spend time in the calm contemplation of your works of art. Cultivate the habit of looking at your trees – it will keep you attuned to their needs.*

garden compost or farm manure to feed bonsai. In theory, either may be used, provided they are well rotted. However there is always a danger of introducing some plant pathogens that, though they may offer no threat to trees in open ground, might prove fatal to a tree confined to a bonsai container.

Soil ingredients

N: Nitrogen Nitrogen is responsible for shoot development and foliage production, in short, for growth. Too little nitrogen results in the plant's failure to thrive, and it will have small, possibly distorted leaves and a washed-out, insipid appearance. With no nitrogen at all, a large plant could die within a year. Too much nitrogen, by contrast, causes rapid growth, with large leaves and plump shoots that are full of water and, consequently, are easy to snap.

P: Phosphorus Phosphorus is essential for the development and proper functioning of roots. It is commonly used in high concentrations for newly potted stock plants and commercial root crops. Phosphorus also encourages the fattening of woody trunks and branches and helps establish appropriate conditions for the production of foliage and flower buds. It also enhances the resistance of plants to stress and disease. Weak growth and a pale colour may be the result of an oversupply, or even a lack, of phosphorus.

K: Potassium Potassium is the main agent for promoting the development of fruit and flowers. Increasing potassium in the diet of bonsai apples or azaleas which fruit or flower poorly, will greatly improve their performance the next spring. Potassium also helps harden late growth to prepare for winter. Insufficient potassium in nonflowering species results in winter die-back. A cheap way to add potassium to soil is to throw a few handfuls of hardwood ash onto the surface.

Trace elements Otherwise known as macro and micro nutrients, trace elements are essential to all plants. They are iron, zinc, copper, boron, magnesium, chlorine, calcium, molybdenum, sulphur and manganese. As they all contribute to a plant's general well-being, a lack of any of these nutrients will be reflected in a lacklustre appearance and performance. Foliage will be pale and growth weak. Sulphur, magnesium and calcium are macro nutrients, which means they are needed in greater amounts than are the other, so-called, micro nutrients.

What type of fertilizer?

Fertilizers come in two kinds: organic (or naturally occurring) and inorganic. Plants are not politically correct – they don't care where their chemical nutrients come from, as long as they get them.

TOP *Organic fertilizer cakes made of rapeseed meal, bonemeal and fish emulsion form the staple diet of most Japanese bonsai. The cakes are placed on the surface of the soil and release nutrients to feed the roots whenever the plants are watered.*

Organic fertilizers One's first instinct would probably be to choose an organic fertilizer, as they break down slowly, releasing their nutrients through the action of microbes in the soil. However, this means that when inert soil mixes (such as akadama, pure peat or grit), are used, organic fertilizers are almost useless until the soil's inherent flora have had time to develop spontaneously.

Once the soil has 'come to life', organic fertilizers will provide a continuous supply of the three basic nutrients plus some trace elements. Some compound organic pellets are NPK-balanced (their relative ratios will be stated on the pack). Other sources are single ingredients such as bone meal, dried blood, rapeseed meal or plain old horse manure. You can use one ingredient, some, or all, individually or in any combination.

While it is difficult to overdose with organic fertilizers, it is also difficult to control the rate of the release of nutrients. Much depends on the weather, as well as the nature of the soil. Many growers use a background feed of fertilizer 'cakes' containing rapeseed meal, bone meal and fish emulsion. They top this up now and again with further applications of synthetic fertilizers, whose nutrient contents are balanced to achieve a specifically desired result (see below).

Synthetic fertilizers Synthetic fertilizers are water soluble and are usually applied at the same time as one waters plants. The nutrients in synthetic fertilizers are immediately available to the roots and function without the need for microbial action. Some are supplied in the form of time-release capsules, with the active ingredients contained within a semi-permeable shell that allows the slow release of nutrients by osmosis each time one waters the plants.

The big advantage of synthetic fertilizers is that it is possible to control precisely how much of the basic nutrients are applied to specific plants, in which proportions, and when. If you are after rapid development, you may increase the amount of nitrogen.

Later in the year, you may wish to increase the amount of phosphorus in order to thicken the trunk and harden off the buds and young roots. You can feed extra potassium if flowering is poor, or to protect young shoots throughout the winter months.

One drawback is that if you water bonsai with a synthetic fertilizer, much of it gets washed away with subsequent watering. This is because of the inert nature of most bonsai soils. Natural, organic garden soils have the capacity to accept nutrients from water, and to hold them within the soil. The fertilizers release foodstuffs only to the plant's roots, and not to the water the next time it rains.

Inert soils have less, or indeed none, of this ability to retain nutrients (known as 'cation exchange capacity' or CEC). The poor CEC of most bonsai soils is the reason why many growers top their plants up with a background feed of a naturally occurring fertilizer. Adding organic matter to soil, other than pure peat (which is inert), markedly increases its CEC.

TOP *Yellowing, as seen here, is a classic sign of magnesium deficiency in old leaves. In young leaves, however, it may be a sign of iron deficiency.*

▶ APPLICATION OF FERTILIZER ◀

When to feed which plant with what?

There's very little point in giving a tree fertilizer it doesn't need, such as within its dormant period. This will do more harm than good. As a rule of thumb, plants require a very generous helping of fertilizer while they are growing vigorously, and none at all when they are not.

A simple method of illustrating the most appropriate feeding programmes is according to the chart below, as plants' requirements differ greatly.

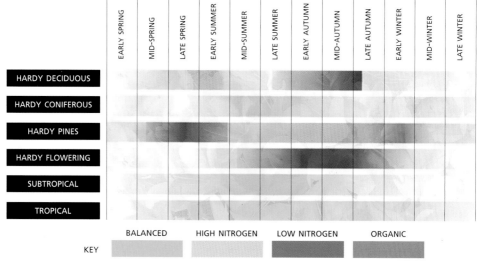

	EARLY SPRING	MID-SPRING	LATE SPRING	EARLY SUMMER	MID-SUMMER	LATE SUMMER	EARLY AUTUMN	MID-AUTUMN	LATE AUTUMN	EARLY WINTER	MID-WINTER	LATE WINTER
HARDY DECIDUOUS												
HARDY CONIFEROUS												
HARDY PINES												
HARDY FLOWERING												
SUBTROPICAL												
TROPICAL												

KEY: BALANCED — HIGH NITROGEN — LOW NITROGEN — ORGANIC

PALER TINTS REPRESENT HALF-STRENGTH DILUTIONS

TOP *Plants take their nutritional requirements from wherever they may find them, so it is possible to feed any combination of organic fertilizers (like the pellets shown here) and inorganic fertilizers. Individual doses should not be too strong.*

Soil application

Organic fertilizers are always applied directly to the soil. They can be mixed in at repotting time, but they are likely to become active too soon for the plant's liking, and may have the effect of 'burning' the new roots.

The best method is to distribute small pellets, cakes or granules over the surface, about 5cm (2in) apart, and evenly spread them over the entire area. Some bonsai nurseries sell plastic mesh baskets to put over the cakes to prevent birds from eating them.

Synthetic fertilizers should be watered into the soil, but never at a higher concentration than the one recommended by the specific manufacturer. A common practice is to apply a quarter-strength solution at each watering over consecutive days.

Foliar application

Plants also absorb synthetic nutrients through their foliage (leaves), often more efficiently than via their roots. As always, follow the manufacturers' instructions, and never foliar feed in direct sunlight, or the leaves will come out in spots,

Some people think that small water droplets act as miniature magnifying glasses that concentrate the sun's rays. This is not the case. It is just that the water is evaporating faster than the nutrients are able to be absorbed, which increases their concentration.

When foliar feeding, use a spray to mist the undersides of leaves as well as their top surfaces. (This is an opportunity to check for pests that might lurk there.)

TOP *The prolific blossom on this Satsuki Azalea was encouraged by the application of a high-potassium fertilizer in mid-summer. Beauty like this is your reward for meticulous attention to a plant's specific needs.*

▶ PESTS AND DISEASES ◀

There are no pests or diseases specific to bonsai. Whatever attacks similar trees in your area will attack your bonsai. Bonsai plants are not any more or any less susceptible to attack by insects or fungal diseases than full-sized trees, but because a bonsai is so small and slow-growing, a variety of diseases and infestations are able to have a more debilitating effect. A small bonsai tree is simply not capable of outgrowing ailments in the way that a more sizable tree might do.

However, thanks to your commitment to watering daily, you have an excellent opportunity to look at your tree while you're doing it, so you're more likely to spot problems that arise before they become serious. If you discover evidence of insect or fungal attack, act at once. Have the problem accurately diagnosed by an expert and seek the most appropriate treatment.

Wherever you live, there will be pests that the staff at your local garden centre are able to help identify. They will also recommend the most effective treatments. Always use products precisely as the manufacturer has indicated on the pack. In many countries, including parts of Europe and the USA, it is illegal not to follow such instructions.

ABOVE *A pine branch infested with aphids. These sap-sucking pests multiply fast, but fortunately are fairly easy to eradicate.*

There are countries where, for example, if I were to recommend using a strong jet of cold water to eradicate, say, spider mites, I would be breaking the law.

Most pesticides and fungicidal preparations are extremely toxic and experimenting with them could prove very dangerous to people as well as to plants. Also, some pests are so common these days that they are, in practical terms, ubiquitous.

Insects

Insects that consume leaves, roots or sap occur naturally, and nature finds a way to achieve a balance between the insect's need for food and the plant's need for leaves and roots. Keeping a tree in a pot upsets the natural balance, which we must restore. Also, there are good and bad insects: some tree-dwelling insects prey on pests. Thoughtless spraying kills them, too.

Aphids These plump sap-suckers multiply at an obscene rate. The first signs of aphid infestation are distorted shoot tips which appear in early summer. Aphids are annoying but are not too difficult to control.

Spider mites Minute creatures that densely colonize foliage, weaving almost imperceptible webs. They suck sap at the base of the leaves and can easily defoliate entire trees. However, they are not too difficult to control.

Galls Many species play host to mites that live in the leaf tissue, where they cause odd-shaped galls. These are usually red and appear on the upper leaf surface, where they look unsightly, but do no harm. Since galls are harmless, little research has been done into their prevention. Snipping off and burning affected leaves early on should keep the tree clear of galls for a year or two.

Root aphids Unlike their cousins, these are not easy to keep under chemical control. Symptoms of root

ABOVE *This maple is infested with gall mites which will soon lead to the development of unsightly red lumps (known as galls) on the leaves.*
TOP *The effect of spider mites on a juniper. These small voracious pests siphon sap from the leaves and are able to defoliate an entire tree.*

Fungi

Fungal problems can be difficult to identify. Sometimes, by the time symptoms are obvious it's too late for treatment, but this is thankfully rare. Prevention though, is better than cure, so good hygiene should not be neglected. Fungal spores are distributed by the wind, and standing water can collect a potent cocktail of them within a short time.

Never spray bonsai with pond water or rain water that has been standing exposed to the air for more than a week. If you store rain-water, keep it covered at all times.

The effects on foliage

Several different fungi may be the cause of the condition called 'black spot'. Most are easily treated, which will stop the spread of the disease, but the spots will remain. Pull off all the infected leaves and burn them.

aphid infestation include a general weakening of the plant, which is hardly ever serious. Hose the roots clean when next you repot, as this is often enough to get rid of this type of pest.

Vine weevils The scourge of container gardeners, these spread fast. The adult, which lays hundreds of eggs, eats notches in the leaves of plants, while the larvae have a voracious appetite for roots. One symptom of infestation is an inexplicable deterioration of the tree. Cure is difficult, as chemical treatments are not freely available to amateurs. Biological controls, like parasitic nematodes, are being marketed and seem effective, but prevention is the best policy. The adult weevil cannot fly, so placing grease bands around the legs of display benches protects trees from attack.

Other insects A myriad tiny, harmless insects suck or burrow in leaves. Either ignore them or, if the tree's appearance is affected, seek advice at a local garden centre.

ABOVE *Some fungal diseases are known as 'rusts' because they manifest as spots of what looks like rust on the leaves.*
TOP *An oak twig with a gall-nut, an ugly protuberance that is caused by gall mites which take up residence inside the leaf tissue.*

ABOVE *Fungi that emerge from lesions in dead wood are often not as harmful as they may seem. If a tree is affected, send a sample to a horticultural research station.*
TOP *Black spot is a disease that may be caused by several types of fungi. The spots will remain, even after successful treatment.*

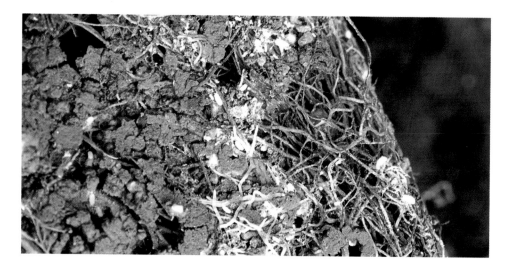

Mycorrhizae: the beneficial fungus

This fungus appears as white or cream fibres intermingled with the roots' tips. The picture above, which depicts a colony of root aphids, looks similar to a crop of the benign fungus. However, close inspection will reveal the insects. Mycorrhizae helps roots to gather nutrients and moisture. This fungus is invaluable; try to re-establish it when repotting by transferring some soil to the new container, along with the burgeoning tree.

Effects on trunks and branches

Various bracket fungi live on dead or, occasionally, on live wood. If the fungi start emerging through live bark, remove them at once and send them off to a horticultural research station for identification and recommended treatment protocols. Telephone beforehand to get their advice. Remember, the parts that you are able to remove are merely the fruiting bodies of the fungi, the core of the fungus; its mycelium, is still deep inside the tree.

If the fungus arises from dead wood – from sharis or large wounds – the condition might not be serious. Not all fungi that feed on dead wood cause problems, but many do. Rot caused by fungal infection will structurally weaken the tree and might even affect the xylem, too. It won't help to panic, just follow the advice given above.

Effects on roots

A mushroom appearing beside a healthy tree is a harmless gift from nature. However, the more dangerous fungi are usually not seen. Waterlogged, poorly aerated soil provides a great environment for root-rotting fungi whose spores float in air. Manure or compost may harbour spores, so don't use them to enrich soil.

Symptoms of root fungi are discoloured foliage, wilting, and die-back of new shoots. The best way to deal with it is to repot, using open, friable soil.

Cultivating healthy habits

Health problems are far better prevented than cured. Good hygiene and regular inspections should be a part of your routine. When you water your trees daily, examine each of them in turn so that you will be able to spot even the slightest of changes almost as soon as they occur. The following check list will help you develop healthy habits:

○ Before you water, make sure the tree actually needs it. If the soil is damp, don't water. If it is bone dry, ensure that it doesn't dry out again. If it rains for days, tilt the pots at an angle to encourage drainage.

○ Check the foliage and shoots for anything unusual: an odd colour, distorted leaves, wilting etc. Drying winds and/or hot sun cause species like maples and hornbeams to develop dry leaf-margins; if this occurs, move the trees to a more sheltered spot.

○ Strip disfigured leaves and try to discover the cause. Examine shoots and foliage for aphids and, if you see any signs, treat immediately.

○ Check the inner areas, especially of conifers, for dry or dead leaves. This may be natural wastage, but could also be caused by spider mites. Remove dead leaves. While you're at it, clear the inner areas of debris.

○ If some foliage is sick, but the rest of the plant is in good health, find out why. There may be a tight wire, or a branch might have been damaged at a fork or where it meets the trunk. Or, the roots directly below one or other of the branches may have died off.

○ Check trees for the telltale white specks left by scale insects, and scrape them off.

○ While you're looking for signs of insect damage, check that wires are not digging into the bark. If any wires seem tight, cut them away.

○ Clean the soil surface, removing fallen leaves or debris that might harbour spores or bugs. This is important in the autumn and winter.

○ Are organic fertilizer cakes breaking down? If not, put some earth or a piece of fresh moss around each cake to introduce microbes. Don't worry about cakes that seem to be growing hairs or those full of worms: this is part of the natural process and will do no harm.

○ Is your tree vigorous? If not, are you feeding it adequately? Is the soil too wet, or too dry? Don't automatically feed or water again until you are sure what is causing problems, or you might make things worse.

○ Do any shoots need pinching back? During summer, broadleaved trees grow almost all the time and it is essential to keep the pinching under control. Junipers, too, grow all the time and it is a good idea to pinch out the new tips daily, right through to mid-autumn.

○ In winter, check all trees at least once a week to make sure the soil is moist and that there is no evidence of pests.

○ Finally, stand back and take pleasure in the admiration of each of your trees in turn: this is what bonsai trees are for! Visualize the possible future development of each of them and think about the most likely route you will take to achieve that objective, until the final, near-perfect image is firmly fixed in your mind.

KEEPING YOUR BONSAI
IN SHAPE
Tools, pinching, pruning and wiring

Specialist bonsai tools can be expensive, and the top of the range equipment falls into the category of hedonistic luxury. One should invest in good basic equipment. As the bonsai novice will soon discover, the points of the most costly brushed stainless-steel shears break off every bit as easily as do the tips of ordinary ones. On the other hand, the very cheapest tools are not even worth the small amount of money spent on them, as they tend to be fragile and badly made. Tools like this don't keep a good edge for long, nor do they fulfil their function adequately.

▸ TOOLS AND EQUIPMENT ◂

For one's first foray into bonsai, it is possible to get by with ordinary household tools, while slowly building up a proper kit of specialized tools and equipment. To start, you'll need just the basics depicted on the following pages.

In addition to this starter kit, there are a few other bits and pieces you might find useful: a turntable is invaluable when working with bonsai, a cake decorator's turntable or something salvaged from an old record player will be fine. A small curved trowel is handy for adding soil to the pot, make one from an old tin can. A scalpel or modelling knife is also useful for cleaning up pruning wounds on roots and branches. An old toothbrush comes in handy for gentle scrubbing. So do strips of rubber, which can be strategically placed to protect the bark from wire pressure. Sieves are handy for removing particles from the soil.

You'll need wire for training branches. Aluminium wire is the easiest to manipulate,

but it is not readily available, although some garden suppliers do sell it. The green plastic-covered iron wire that is sold for garden use is far too stiff, as is all iron wire, and you could damage delicate branches when you apply it.

Copper wire is excellent and is always used in Japan for conifers, as not only does it become work-hardened but it is stronger than aluminium wire. For deciduous trees, most Japanese growers use aluminium wire, but copper is just as effective. Copper wire can be salvaged from off-cuts of electrical cable, from which the plastic insulation can be scraped or burned. You'll find copper wire easier to use if it is annealed. This process makes the wire softer by aligning the molecules, which are then re-aligned, making the wire stiffer once it has been applied. To anneal copper wire: heat it till it is red hot, and allow it to cool slowly. When the wire has cooled, it will take on a dull, rusty colour. In some cases it might

OPPOSITE *Bonsai tools range from ordinary household items to a few highly specialized implements. Using the right tools definitely makes it easier to achieve the desired results.*

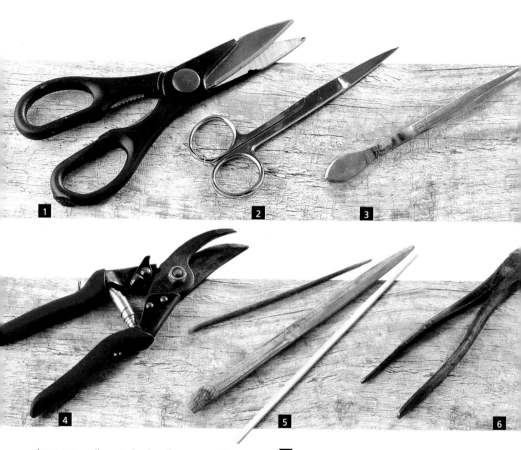

become a vibrant shade of orange. However, this is just surface oxidation which will come off as soon as the wire is handled. It will now be much softer than it was before. The change can be assessed by gently flexing the piece of wire a few times. The more vigorously you flex it, the stiffer it will become.

BASIC TOOLS

1 **STURDY SCISSORS** FOR CUTTING ROOTS. THESE NEED TO BE VERY SHARP, AS ROOTS CAN BE FIBROUS AND TOUGH.

2 **SMALL SCISSORS** FOR CUTTING SHOOTS; THESE MUST ALSO BE SHARP. SURGICAL OR NAIL SCISSORS ARE PERFECT FOR THE JOB.

3 **A PAIR OF TWEEZERS** FOR A MULTITUDE OF TASKS; FROM PICKING OFF BUGS TO WEEDING SMALL POTS.

4 **SECATEURS** OF THE 'BYPASS' TYPE ('ANVIL' SECATEURS WILL CRUSH THE BARK AND MAKE CLOSE CUTTING AWKWARD). A SMALL PAIR WITH NEAT, NARROW JAWS CAN BE USED EVEN IN TIGHT CORNERS.

5 **KNITTING NEEDLE OR WOODEN CHOPSTICK** FOR COMBING OUT ROOTS. YOU CAN ALSO USE A WOODEN KEBAB STICK OR A CHOPSTICK TO TEST FOR MOISTURE IN A POT (SEE P54).

6 **WIRE CUTTERS** LIGHT TYPES ARE BETTER THAN HEAVY INDUSTRIAL ONES, AND ARE EASIER TO MANIPULATE IN AWKWARD SPOTS.

Specialist tools

There's no doubt that specialist bonsai tools make the job easier and give better results. The best way to build up your collection of tools is to acquire them one by one, on a need-to-use basis. The tools pictured here are the main weapons in the bonsai growers' arsenal. Some of them are equally useful in general gardening as well, so you can get twice the benefit from your investment.

SPECIALIST TOOLS

1 **TWIG SHEARS** UNLIKE SCISSORS, THE BLADES OF THESE SHEARS ARE VERY SHARP AND THEY TAPER TO POINTS. THEY CAN BE USED FOR TWIGS, SHOOTS AND LEAF STALKS; THE FINELY-POINTED TIPS ENABLE INTRICATE CUTS TO BE MADE ACCURATELY.

2 **ANGLED CUTTER** THIS IS THE MOST USEFUL TOOL TO START WITH. THE ANGLED CUTTING EDGE MAKES IT POSSIBLE TO CUT NEATLY, FLUSH WITH THE TRUNK AND INTO THE FORKS OF BRANCHES. ONCE YOU'VE USED ANGLED CUTTERS, YOU'LL DITCH YOUR USUAL SECATEURS AND USE THESE IN THE GARDEN AS WELL.

3 **CONCAVE CUTTERS** SIMILAR TO ANGLED CUTTERS BUT WITH A CURVED CUTTING EDGE. DESIGNED FOR PRUNING BRANCH STUBS, THESE LEAVE A HOLLOW WOUND WHICH HEALS TOTALLY FLAT

Optional extras

There are a few odds and ends that will come in handy only now and again, so your bonsai toolbox is bound to put on weight as the years progress. These include turntables and gouges, electric carving knives, jin-scrapers and various round-nosed and other pliers.

Most of these may only be needed once or twice a year – but are absolutely invaluable when you do need them.

Care of tools

Always keep tools clean and sharp. Dirty tools become stiff to use and carry disease from tree to tree. Learning to sharpen tools, especially those with curved cutting edges, takes practice. A fine oilstone is good for honing, and a diamond-impregnated finishing stone makes for a keen edge. Note how the cutting edges of the tools don't meet exactly – one passes beneath the other. This ensures that the through-cut is complete and that the edges don't blunt each other as they cut. Tools may be cleaned with white spirit or hand-cleaner.

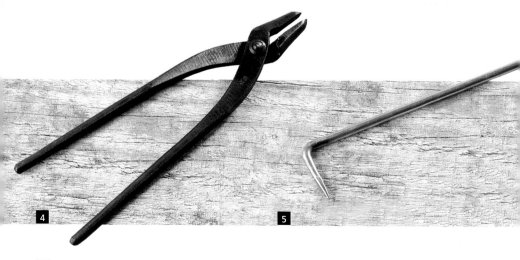

4 **JIN PLIERS** NAMED FOR THEIR USEFULNESS WHEN STRIPPING BARK TO MAKE *JINS* (SEE P146). THESE ARE EQUALLY USEFUL FOR HANDLING WIRE – NOTE THEIR DELICATE JAWS.

5 **ROOT HOOK** YOU CAN MAKE ONE OF THESE USEFUL TOOLS FROM A LENGTH OF MILD STEEL ROD.

6 **WIRE CUTTERS** THESE ARE A CUT ABOVE ORDINARY WIRE CUTTERS. THE LONG HANDLES FACILITATE GETTING INTO AWKWARD AREAS TO REMOVE WIRE, AND THE SHORT, SNUB-NOSED JAWS CUT TAUT WIRES WITHOUT DOING DAMAGE TO THE BARK.

7 **ROOT SHEARS** A STURDIER VERSION OF TWIG SHEARS. KEEPING A SPECIAL TOOL FOR CUTTING TOUGH, SOIL-COVERED ROOTS MEANS YOUR REGULAR SHEARS RETAIN THEIR KEEN EDGE!

8 **BRANCH CLAMPS** SIMPLE DEVICES FOR INTRODUCING ACUTE BENDS IN THICK OR SHORT BRANCHES, WHERE WIRES WOULD NOT BE EFFECTIVE.

9 **WIRE BRUSH** SOFT BRASS FILAMENTS CAN BE USED TO CLEAN UP TRUNKS AND BRANCHES, AS WELL AS DEADWOOD AREAS.

10 **ROOT RAKE AND TWEEZERS** USELESS FOR REPOTTING, THE RAKE IS ACTUALLY DESIGNED FOR WEEDING THE POTS. THE HANDLE MAY ALSO BE USED IN PLACE OF A SECOND PAIR OF TWEEZERS.

11 **PRUNING SAW** SPECIALLY DESIGNED FOR BONSAI USE, WITH A THIN BLADE AND FINE TEETH. THESE CUT ON THE PULL STROKE, WHICH IS LESS LIKELY TO SHRED DELICATE BARK.

12 WIRE SPECIALIST BONSAI NURSERIES STOCK ALUMINIUM WIRE IN A RANGE OF SIZES FROM 1MM TO 6MM (1/24–1/4IN). IN THE SMALLER SIZES, THE INCREASES ARE IN 0.5MM (.0197IN) INCREMENTS. STOCK UP WITH A LARGE COIL OF ONE OR TWO SIZES FOR YOUR IMMEDIATE REQUIREMENTS, ADDING OTHER SIZES AS YOU NEED TO. BUYING SMALL COILS IS EXPENSIVE IN THE LONG RUN.

13 PLASTIC MESH THIS IS ESSENTIAL FOR COVERING DRAINAGE HOLES.

▶ PRUNING ◀

Pruning is done for three reasons: to remove unwanted branches, to maintain an established form, or to encourage new growth close to the trunk. In bonsai, it is essential to make the wounds as neat and as unobtrusive as possible, so they won't spoil the good looks of an otherwise attractive tree.

Pruning cuts should be sealed immediately, preferably with Japanese cut paste. This is a putty-like substance that keeps the cut edge moist, which helps to prevent the surrounding tissue from contracting. If you can't find cut paste at your nursery, you could use ordinary children's synthetic modelling clay, mixed with a little olive oil to stop it from hardening. Once the edges of the wound have begun to 'roll in'

the paste can be removed. Never use bitumen-based pruning compounds. These dry black and hard, disfiguring the tree.

The timing of pruning varies according to the reason for doing it. Branch pruning is best done in autumn; maintenance pruning takes place in late winter or early spring; and regenerative pruning is done in mid-summer, when the tree is growing at its fastest possible rate.

How wounds heal

Wounds on trees and other plants don't heal in the same way as they might if the trauma were caused to an animal. That is to say, trees are not able to repair damaged tissue. Instead, they patiently set about manufacturing a new layer each year, until the wound is entirely covered over. The length of time this process takes will depend upon the size and nature of the wound and the relative thickness of each new annual ring.

COVERING A PRUNING WOUND

 BARK

NEW RINGS AFTER PRUNING

PRUNING WOUND

ABOVE *This shows how layers of new wood laid down each year gradually cover a pruning wound. In this example, it took five years to cover the scar, and has grown on for another two. It is easy to see how leaving a small stub would cause an ugly swelling as the wound heals.*

TOP *Japanese cut paste is used to good effect to minimize the scar which is beginning to form on the trunk of this bonsai maple. The special compound acts by keeping the edges of pruning wounds moist, so that neat healing is encouraged.*

ABOVE LEFT *After two to three years, carefully executed pruning wounds gradually become completely covered over with fresh woody tissue.*

ABOVE RIGHT *Careless pruning might cause the surrounding tissue to contract, leaving a larger, more unsightly scar than is absolutely necessary.*

▶ REMOVING BRANCHES ◀

Once you have spent time observing and getting to know your tree really well, you will start to perceive new ways to make sensitive improvements to it. Most mass-produced, commercial bonsai are burdened with too many branches, so they get to look unpleasantly congested. Removing a few selected branches opens up the structure of the tree. This has the effect of providing more space for the remaining branches to expand into, which is good for both its health and its appearance. Remember, always, that bonsai is a visual discipline whose end result should be a living work of art.

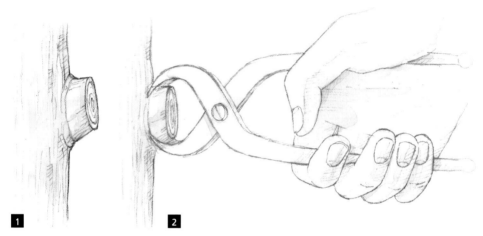

1

2

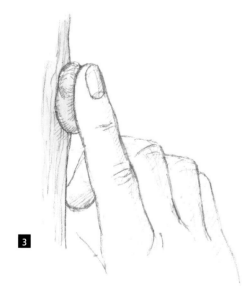

3

REMOVING A BRANCH

1 FIRST, CUT THROUGH THE UNWANTED BRANCH CLOSE TO THE TRUNK, USING SECATEURS OR ANGLED CUTTERS. THICK BRANCHES ARE BEST CUT WITH A FINE SAW.

2 THEN USE A CONCAVE CUTTER TO REMOVE THE STUB. DO THIS IN STAGES TO BEGIN WITH. MAKE THE FINAL CUT SO THAT THE WOUND IS HOLLOW, BUT BE CAREFUL NOT TO MAKE IT WIDER THAN NECESSARY. IF YOU DO NOT POSSESS A CONCAVE CUTTER, USE A SHARP MODELLING KNIFE TO CLEAN UP THE WOUND. A CURVED CUTTING EDGE HELPS WITH THE HOLLOWING OUT. BE CAREFUL NOT TO LET THE SHARP BLADE SLIP. USING YOUR FREE HAND, BRACE THE HAND THAT IS HOLDING THE KNIFE FIRMLY AGAINST THE TRUNK.

3 ONCE YOU HAVE HOLLOWED THE WOUND, APPLY A PLUG OF JAPANESE OR HOME-MADE CUT PASTE. IF YOU DO NOT HAVE THESE, YOU CAN USE PVA WOOD GLUE OR EVEN BATHROOM MASTIC, ALTHOUGH NEITHER IS IDEAL, AS THEY TEND TO STICK ALL TOO WELL.

▶ GENERATING NEW GROWTH ◀

When building branches from scratch, or if you decide you want to remodel parts of your tree, you'll need to generate new shoots from thick branches that are several years old. Sometimes, when developing a Broom Style for example, you'll need to cut right through the trunk. This can be done to almost all broadleaved trees with virtually total success, but never do this to a conifer. Conifers are not able to generate new growth from old, leafless branches.

The best time to encourage a tree to generate new growth is in midsummer, when the tree is in full growth. The sudden elimination of all the foliage-bearing twigs in one area will stimulate masses of new shoots from within the cambium layer; many more than you are ever likely to need.

GENERATING NEW GROWTH

1 DECIDE WHERE YOU WANT THE BRANCH TO FORK INTO TWO OR THREE SMALLER BRANCHES AND CUT STRAIGHT THROUGH WITH A FINE SAW OR AN ANGLED CUTTER. USE PASTE TO SEAL THE WOUND, TAKING CARE NOT TO DAMAGE THE TENDER BARK AROUND THE EDGE. SUBSTITUTES FOR CUT PASTE ARE NOT APPROPRIATE HERE, SO IF YOU DON'T HAVE THE PROPER COMPOUND, LEAVE THE WOUND UNSEALED AND ENSURE THAT IT IS PROTECTED FROM THE SUN.

2 A MASS OF NEW BUDS WILL SOON APPEAR IN THE FORM OF A GREEN CROWN ALL AROUND THE CUT END. ALLOW THESE TO GROW ON UNTIL EACH NEW SHOOT HAS THREE OR FOUR LEAVES.

3 ONCE THE SHOOTS HAVE GAINED STRENGTH, IT IS TIME TO SELECT THE ONES YOU WANT TO KEEP, AND TO CUT THE REST AWAY. BE SURE TO CUT THE UNWANTED SHOOTS ALL THE WAY BACK TO THEIR BASES.

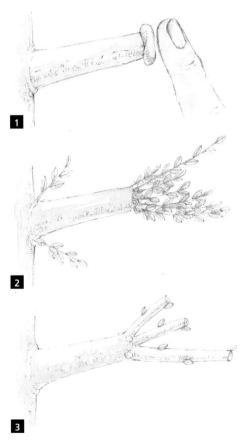

TOP *The large wound inflicted on this trunk has stimulated the underlying cambium to respond by generating dozens of vigorous new shoots.*

▶ MAINTENANCE PRUNING ◀

Once your bonsai has become established and you are happy with the shape, it does not mean that you can stop pruning. This when the business of pruning hots up! The tree must be able to grow each year without altering the balance between roots and foliage, and without spoiling the design.

The annual growth of the tree needs to be under control. If you just nip out the tips of the new shoots year after year, the tree will gradually become too large. Adventitious, sappy shoots growing from the inner branches will become stronger than the heavily-pruned outer twigs, and the tree will be ruined. You will have to start all over again.

Each year you have to reduce the number of outer twigs to allow space for the next year's growth. In addition, every two to four years (depending on the species and size of the bonsai), you have to cut back more vigorously, removing quite old sections of branch, to rebuild the twiggy parts. This may seem drastic, but it has to be done. It will take no more than a year or so for the twigs to become dense again.

Maintenance pruning is best done while the tree is at rest. For conifers, this means late autumn (except junipers), and late winter for broadleaved trees. Junipers respond better to maintenance pruning in the early summer.

PRUNING TO ENCOURAGE NEW GROWTH

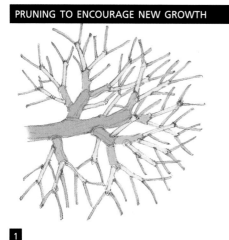

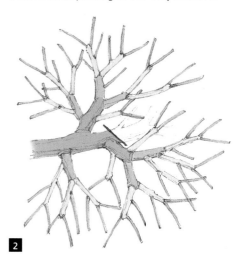

1 THIS SHOWS THE OUTER, TWIGGY AREA OF A TYPICAL ELM BRANCH IN WINTER. LAST SUMMER'S GROWTH IS COLOURED OLIVE GREEN; THE DARKER GREEN IS THE GROWTH THAT FOLLOWED THE SUMMER PINCHING. THE LIGHT BROWN COLOUR REPRESENTS THE PREVIOUS YEAR'S GROWTH AND THE DARKER BROWN IS AT LEAST TWO YEARS OLD. IN ORDER TO MAKE ROOM FOR NEXT YEAR'S SHOOTS, WHILE AT THE SAME TIME PREVENTING THE TREE FROM INCREASING IN SIZE, YOU MUST REDUCE THE NUMBER OF BUDS.

2 CLEAR OUT ANY THICK PARTS WITH TOO MANY OLD SCARS, CUTTING THEM BACK TO A POINT WHERE THERE ARE OTHER, SECONDARY BRANCHLETS. CUT AT AN ANGLE, FOLLOWING THE LINE OF THE SECONDARY BRANCHES. LOOK FOR WAYS TO SHORTEN THE REST OF THE TWIGS, LEAVING THE SAME NUMBER OF BUDS (OR MORE) AS THERE WERE A YEAR AGO. IN THE FIRST ILLUSTRATION, THERE ARE 23 OLIVE GREEN BITS. LEAVE AS MANY BUDS. CUT BACK TO THOSE THAT POINT IN THE DIRECTION YOU WOULD LIKE THE NEW SHOOTS TO GROW, IN ORDER TO FILL ANY VACANT SPACES.

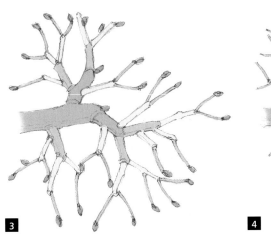

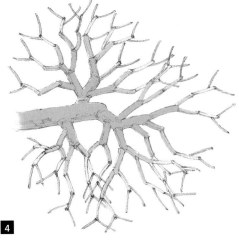

3 PRUNING IS COMPLETE, 28 NEW BUDS (IN BLUE) REMAIN.
WE HAVE CUT BACK TO THE OLDER, DORMANT BUDS.

4 IN THE SPRING, THE BUDS WILL START SPROUTING AND THE
CYCLE WILL BEGIN AGAIN. IN THIS ILLUSTRATION THE GREEN BITS
SHOW (ALL THINGS BEING EQUAL) HOW GROWTH MIGHT
DEVELOP DURING THE FOLLOWING YEAR.

GROWTH FOLLOWING SUMMER PINCHING	PREVIOUS YEAR'S GROWTH
LAST SUMMER'S GROWTH	GROWTH 2 YEARS PRIOR TO THAT

TOP *When pruning pines, look carefully between the pairs or groups of needles, because
this is where the buds develop. Take care of the tiny buds which may appear on otherwise
bare branches; you might have need of their shoots in a year or two.*

Pruning the outer areas

The idea here is to remove some of the shoots that grew in the summer and to shorten others, so that you leave about the same number of buds as there were a year ago. If some areas seem somewhat sparse, you can leave a few more buds. In areas that are too dense, leave fewer.

Some species have opposing leaves (e.g. maple) and others, alternate leaves (e.g. zelkova). Species with opposite leaves have more buds at the internodes. Species such as pines and junipers have no regular pattern of bud location.

Thinning branches

This is like pruning the outer areas but on a larger scale. One selects twigs and branches for removal, rather than shoots and buds. First, cut off thick sections of outer branches, so that younger, side branches may grow on to replace them.

ABOVE *The tips of a Chinese Juniper (Shimpaku) can be pinched throughout the growing season.*

TOP *A Japanese Red Maple* (Acer palmatum 'chishio') *just prior to its regular winter pruning.*
ABOVE *The same Japanese Red Maple after it has been carefully and sensitively pruned.*

Trees grow each year, either in one or two summer surges, or more or less continually, depending on the species and climate. The object of pinching shoots as they grow is to keep the foliage areas neat, reduce the size of the leaves, and make small twigs denser. Each time you pinch a shoot, new ones grow from the buds at the base of each remaining leaf and, probably, from other places as well. So pinching is a bit like having a haircut; it all has to grow back for a while before any improvement becomes obvious.

The root system of the tree can support a maximum total area of the leaf surface, so the more leaves there are, the smaller they will be. Naturally, more shoots means more leaves. So when you pinch out one shoot, encouraging the plant to produce two more, the new leaves will tend to be somewhat smaller, of course.

The timing depends on the stage of development of the tree. If you want to start building dense twigs, allow the shoots to grow until they begin to change colour, and then cut them back almost to the base. Leave one or two leaves on broadleaved trees, and six or seven clusters of needles on pines. (Chinese Junipers are always dense, so don't worry about them.) Pinching will make the next crop of shoots strong and vigorous. If you already have quite dense twigs, you can pinch broadleaved trees as soon as the shoot has developed an internode leaf, or pair of leaves. The timing for pines is explained on page 90. Chinese Junipers can be pinched at any time.

ABOVE *The dense, fine twigs on this beautiful Bird's Nest Spruce (*Picea abies var. nidiformis*) were built and maintained by a judicious combination of winter pruning and summer pinching. The bonsai was developed from a humble field specimen.*

► PINCHING TECHNIQUES ◄

Pines

Pines are unique in the way the shoots grow and in how they respond to pinching. The shoot does not bear leaves (or needles), as it grows, each opening from a terminal bud. The bud extends with small, embryonic needles pressed flat against a thick shoot. Only when the shoot is almost at its fullest extent do the needles get larger and start to peel away. Furthermore, wherever you cut through the current year's pine shoot, it will form a small cluster of buds at that point.

No other tree does this. A pine might also produce buds on the sides of a shoot, and on older parts as well. Timing affects the type, the location and to an extent, the nature of new buds that will follow. Early pinching stimulates fat buds at the tips and elsewhere, but seldom on the older twigs. Pinching when the shoots are semi-mature and completely green stimulates more, and smaller, buds. Some buds will also make their appearance on old wood.

If you wait until the needles are already peeling away from the shoot and lie at about 45° and then cut the shoot almost to its base, many more buds will appear on older parts of the branches and all round the base of that shoot. This technique is used to prepare young branchlets for use when one is restructuring the outer areas.

At whatever stage you pinch, bear in mind that the top is likely to be more vigorous than the lower branches. Pinch the weaker parts of the tree first. Then the frailer shoots on the rest of the tree and finally, the most vigorous ones. The whole process should be timed to take ten days. This ensures that the hormones that stimulate new buds reach the weak parts before the stronger ones get their heads in the trough!

ABOVE *These tiny buds are growing on a section of branch that is over 10 years old. They were stimulated by cutting through the new shoots in late summer, after they had almost matured.*

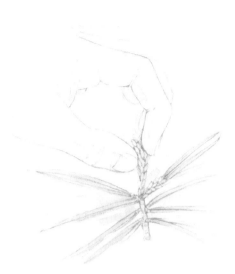

Pinch pine 'candles' (above) by gripping them between thumb and forefinger, simultaneously pulling and twisting slightly. Pinching the candles while they are still young causes new buds to form at the tips and one or two might form further back along the branch. Cutting the shoots once the needles are semi-mature causes more buds to form, especially on older wood. However, these will tend to be small and frail and may not develop fully for a year or two.

Chinese Junipers

Chinese Junipers (*Juniperus chinensis var. sargentii*) have scale foliage when adult, and the juvenile, needle-like foliage only when they are young, or if they have been mistreated in some way. These juvenile shoots should be cut off as soon as they appear – unless the whole tree looks like this – when you must wait for a year or two until it settles into its adult foliage.

In junipers, the adult foliage grows in elongating 'feathers' or fans. Each of the dense shoots is constantly in the process of extending. The central ones elongate faster, becoming plumper and brighter in colour. If you neglect your pinching, the Chinese Juniper will swell like an inflating balloon, and it could take years to get it back into shape.

TOP RIGHT *Juniper foliage is always dense, and pinching becomes an almost daily activity. Bonsai like these can be time-consuming – an aspect worth bearing in mind when you make your initial choice of tree species.*

Other conifers

Hinoki Cypress (*Chamaecyparis obtusa*) are sometimes available as bonsai. These are very much like Chinese junipers (*Juniperus chinensis var. sargentii*) and they should be treated in much the same way.

Needle Junipers (*Juniperus rigida*) and Temple Cedars (*Cryptomeria japonica*) are also used for commercial bonsai, but not in any great numbers. They are also among the most difficult to keep.

If you are growing your own bonsai, there are conifer species which are excellent for the purpose, such as varieties of larch (*Larix*), spruce (*Picea*), yew (*Taxus*), etc. All these species produce visible buds on the shoots, so you pinch them in more or less the same way you would those of any broadleaved tree.

The only major difference is that you would pinch back to a selected bud, rather than to a leaf. If you raise the shoot and look at the under-side, the tiny buds are easier to spot.

PINCHING JUNIPER LEAVES

1 TO PINCH THE DENSE FOLIAGE OF A CHINESE JUNIPER, GRIP A TUFT OF FOLIAGE BETWEEN THE THUMB AND FOREFINGER OF ONE HAND, PULLING OFF THE TIPS WITH THE OTHER HAND (ABOVE). CUTTING WITH SCISSORS WILL JUST CAUSE THE ENDS TO GO BROWN.

2 IT IS ESSENTIAL FOR THE HEALTH OF THE TREE TO CUT BACK THE FATTER, ELONGATING SHOOTS RIGHT TO THE HEALTHY, BRIGHT GREEN LATERAL GROWTH (BELOW).

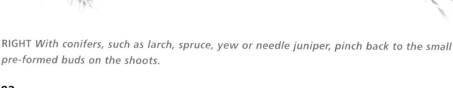

RIGHT *With conifers, such as larch, spruce, yew or needle juniper, pinch back to the small pre-formed buds on the shoots.*

ABOVE *Conifers like the Temple Cedar (*Cryptomeria japonica*) make stunning bonsai once you get the hang of caring for them. With regular pinching, the foliage becomes dense and the needles reduce in length to only 6mm (1/4in).*

Broadleaved trees

When you are developing a new bonsai, you need to increase the density of the twigs. Let the shoots grow freely until they have three or four internodes (the spaces between leaves or pairs of leaves), then cut them all back at once, leaving just a few buds.

Choose the number of buds, and the direction of the bud at the tip, according to the way you want the twigs to develop. Once you are happy with the density you've achieved, the technique changes, because now you will need to maintain the form and encourage the plant to develop smaller leaves. Wait until one internode has appeared on the new shoot and then pinch out the terminal bud. (This is very easy to do with a pair of tweezers.)

The procedure described above discourages any further elongation of the first internode, although it does promote the production of smaller leaves (as the first leaves to appear on a new shoot are usually the smallest ones).

DEVELOPING TWIG DENSITY

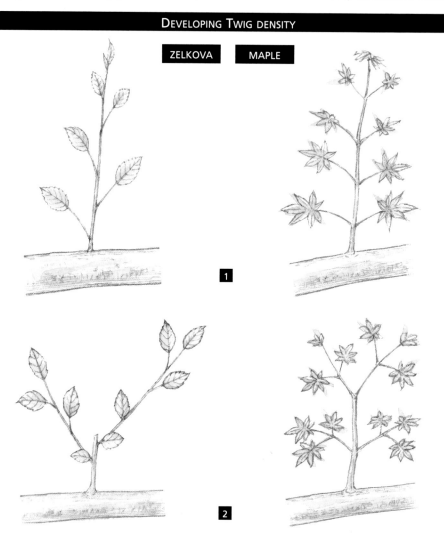

ZELKOVA   MAPLE

1

2

Developing twig density

1 (ILLUSTRATED LEFT, USING A
MAPLE AND A ZELKOVA)

TO STIMULATE THE DEVELOPMENT OF
A MASS OF FINE TWIGS, ALLOW THE
SHOOTS TO GROW UNTIL THEY EACH
HAVE FOUR OR FIVE INTERNODES.
(NOTE: A MAPLE SHOOT HAS TWICE
AS MANY LEAVES PER INTERNODE AS
A ZELKOVA.) CUT BACK THE
SHOOTS, LEAVING A FEW BUDS; HOW
MANY WILL DEPEND UPON YOUR
EVENTUAL AIM.

2 AFTER A WEEK OR TWO, NEW
SHOOTS WILL GROW FROM THE
REMAINING BUDS, AND OFTEN FROM
THE BASE OF THE SHOOT AS WELL.

Leaf pruning

If you decide to show
your tree in an exhibition,
there is a leaf pruning
technique that can be
employed on broadleaved
trees to promote extra-fine
twigs for winter display; or
to stimulate a fresh crop of
smaller leaves for summer
display. This should only be
done on established bonsai
(and never in consecutive
years, as there is a risk of
weakening the tree).

As it is not practical to
leaf prune much later than
mid-summer, plan ahead.

LEAF PRUNING

BUDS

LEAF STALKS

1 (ILLUSTRATED ABOVE RIGHT) CUT OFF THE LEAVES. DO
NOT PULL THEM OFF, AS THIS DAMAGES THE BUDS AT THE BASE
OF THE STALKS. LEAVING STALKS INTACT PROTECTS THE BUDS.

2 NEW BUDS WILL SPROUT WITHIN 2–3 WEEKS, PRODUCING
A CROP OF SMALL BRIGHT LEAVES TO GIVE COLOUR IN THE
AUTUMN.

Flowering bonsai

Flowering bonsai should be treated quite differently. If you pinch them as you would other trees it will have the effect of halting the smooth production of flower buds. The best practice therefore, would probably be to try to delay the regular winter pruning until after flowering has finished, and then prune as you would any other tree. Allow any new growth to continue until late summer and then cut all the shoots back to no more than two or three buds. If you examine them closely, you'll notice that these buds are rounder and plumper than the others, as they are the flower buds that are preparing to burst into glorious bloom next spring.

THE FATTER BUDS AT THE BASE OF THIS SHOOT ARE THE FLOWER BUDS. PRUNE BACK TO THESE ONLY IN THE LATE SUMMER.

Azalea

The sole exception to the rules that govern the pruning of flowering bonsai is the azalea. Azalea flowers, which come in a range of brilliant shades and colours, are borne at the tips of the previous year's shoots, so do not prune these in late summer, or you will have no show!

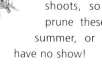

ABOVE *Azalea flowers are borne at the tips of the previous year's growth.*

Wire training techniques allow you to position branches and twigs precisely, and to introduce curves into thin trunks. There is no real substitute for training with wires, apart from more invasive methods which involve moving branches. The possible alternatives, which are dealt with at the end of this section, are both imprecise and time-consuming.

The principle behind wiring could not be simpler. Wire of an appropriate thickness is coiled round the entire length of a trunk or branch. The branch is then bent and manipulated into position. Provided that the wire is applied correctly and is strong enough, it will hold the branch firmly in the desired new position. After some time, which is subject to great variation depending on species and season, the branch will 'set' in the right place and the wires may be removed.

There is one hazard that is best avoided. As the branch grows, it will thicken until eventually the wire begins to bite into the bark. This can happen in just a few weeks, so be vigilant! Immediately the wire begins to cause a dent in the bark, cut it away. Don't attempt to uncoil it unless there is no other option. The action of uncoiling wires puts undue stress on the branches and may break them.

What sort of wire to use

Aluminium wire is the best to start with, because it is easy to apply. Copper wire, once it has been annealed (see p77), is slightly stiffer than aluminium, but becomes much stiffer once it has been applied, giving it superb 'holding power'. Ferrous wire is far too rigid; also, when it weathers, there is a risk that unsightly rust might stain the bark of your tree.

ABOVE *For wire to work effectively it must be both well anchored and carefully applied. Properly applied wires will hold a branch securely in its new position until it sets there permanently.*

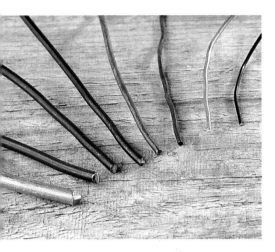

Before you let yourself loose on your precious bonsai, practise your wiring skills on a garden shrub. Test the twig for resistance, then coil the wire at an angle of about 45°. It should be tight enough to make contact with the bark all round, but no tighter. Bend the twig to see if the wire is strong enough to hold it. Before long you'll be able to assess what thickness of wire to use for any given thickness of branch or twig.

INCORRECT AND CORRECT WIRING

A THIS WIRING IS TOO CLOSELY COILED AND WILL RESTRICT THE FLOW OF SAP, WHICH MAY KILL THE BRANCH.

B HERE, THE WIRING IS TOO OPEN, AND WILL NOT HAVE SUFFICIENT HOLDING POWER.

C THIS WIRE IS TOO LOOSE, AND WILL HAVE NO EFFECT AT ALL ON THE BRANCH.

D PERFECT WIRING. THE WIRE IS IN GENTLE CONTACT WITH THE BRANCH AND IS EVENLY SPIRALLED AT 45°.

How wiring works

As a tree grows, it lays down fresh layers of sapwood, or xylem. The new layers of xylem will conform to the shape you have imposed on a branch. Once the new layers become stronger than the original wood, the branch will set. Young shoots that are still green have no significant wood to resist being bent; so they set in position within just a few weeks. Older branches have laid down many layers of wood and will resist being bent, so they take longer to set.

When bending very thick branches it is difficult to avoid damaging the bark and the underlying woody tissues. This may result in the bark splitting on the outside of a curve, or in its compression on the inside of the curve. This should not cause problems, as trees have a way of recovering from such stress. Indeed, scar tissue formed in this way can help a branch to set.

To be on the safe side though, as soon as you see (or hear) a crack, stop bending the branch! If you must bend it even further, wait about a month before you do so.

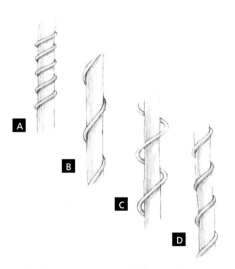

TOP The wire used for bonsai comes in a range of eight thicknesses which vary from 6mm (1/4in) to 1mm (1/24in). The best is aluminium wire, as it is both strong and gentle to delicate bark.

▸ WIRING TRUNKS ◂

If you start with a tree young enough to have a flexible trunk, you will have all the leeway you need for the introduction of interesting shapes. Also, should you wish to shorten the trunk, you could just cut the top back to a young branch, which would then be wired and bent upwards to replace the former apex.

The more often you repeat the process of shortening the leading shoot and wiring in a replacement, the more movement will be achieved in the trunk line and the greater will be the taper. Patience in the early stages will pay off handsomely in the long term.

ABOVE *In addition to adding curves to a trunk, wiring may be employed to make a trunk straighter, if that is what you wish to achieve.*

WIRING A NEW APEX

1 FIRST CUT OFF THE OLD APEX JUST ABOVE A FLEXIBLE YOUNG BRANCH. MAKE THE CUT AT THE REAR, WHERE IT WON'T BE SEEN, CUTTING AT A FAIRLY STEEP ANGLE, SO THAT YOU ARE ABLE TO CREATE A SMOOTH TRANSITION.

2 SECURE THE WIRE ON THE LOWER TRUNK BY COILING IT AROUND FOR AT LEAST THREE COMPLETE TURNS; THEN CONTINUE TO COIL IT ALONG THE BRANCH. MAKE SURE THAT THE FIRST COIL OF WIRE PASSES UNDERNEATH THE BASE OF THE BRANCH. THIS WILL HELP TO HOLD IT IN POSITION WITHOUT SPLITTING THE BARK.

3 FINALLY, MANOEUVRE THE BRANCH UPWARDS, SO THAT IT CONTINUES THE PATTERN OF CURVES ESTABLISHED IN THE LOWER TRUNK. IN A FEW YEARS IT WILL BE IMPOSSIBLE TO DETECT WHAT YOU'VE DONE. IF ONE STRAND OF WIRE IS NOT STRONG ENOUGH TO MAINTAIN THE BEND, APPLY ANOTHER ALONGSIDE THE FIRST. THE SECOND WIRE DOESN'T HAVE TO CONTINUE ALL THE WAY TO THE APEX IF IT IS NOT NEEDED TO HOLD THE BEND ON THE THINNER PART OF THE TRUNK.

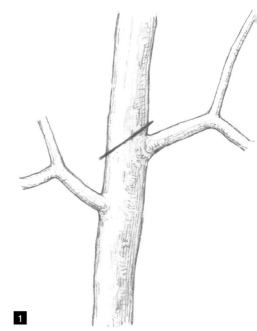

1

WIRING A TRUNK

1 START BY JUDGING WHETHER THE WIRE IS THICK ENOUGH TO DO THE JOB. CUT A PIECE OF WIRE ABOUT ONE-THIRD LONGER THAN THE TRUNK. ANCHOR THE WIRE BY PUSHING ONE END INTO THE SOIL AT THE BASE OF THE TRUNK, RIGHT DOWN TO THE BOTTOM OF THE SHALLOW POT. TRY NOT TO DAMAGE TOO MANY ROOTS WHILE YOU DO THIS. WITH ONE HAND, HOLD THE WIRE FIRMLY TO THE BASE OF THE TRUNK. WITH THE OTHER HAND, BEGIN TO COIL THE WIRE AT A 45° ANGLE. AFTER EACH TURN, MOVE THE HAND THAT'S KEEPING THE WIRE TAUT UPWARDS SO IT FOLLOWS THE SPIRAL AS IT COILS ITS WAY UP THE TRUNK

2 IF THE TRUNK BECOMES TOO THIN FOR THE WIRE YOU'RE USING, CHANGE TO A FINER STRAND. OVERLAP THE WIRES BY AT LEAST TWO FULL TURNS.

3 BEND THE TRUNK WITH BOTH YOUR HANDS, USING YOUR THUMBS AS FULCRUMS. MAKE THE CURVES NARROWER TOWARDS THE TOP. REMEMBER, A TREE IS THREE-DIMENSIONAL, SO IT SHOULD BE EQUALLY BENT BACKWARDS AND FORWARDS AS WELL AS FROM SIDE TO SIDE.

1

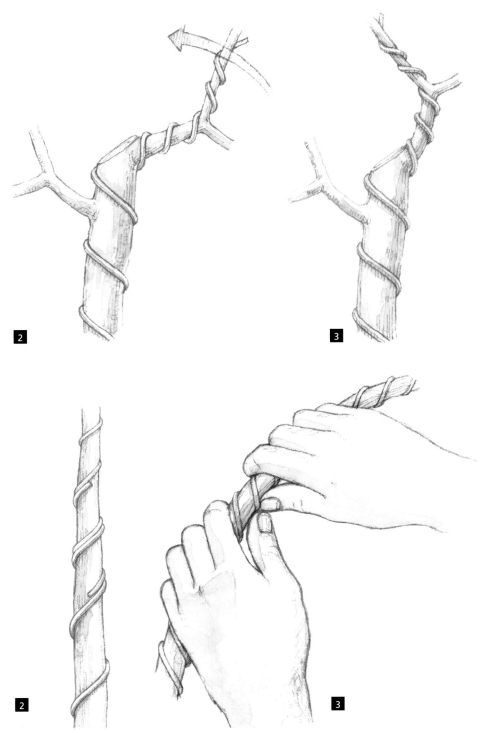

▶ WIRING BRANCHES ◀

The biggest problem when wiring branches is to avoid using too much wire. Not only would this look awful, but it would also tend to restrict the flow of sap and might well damage the branch permanently. It may even prove fatal.

You need to work out a strategy in advance. Where it is feasible, use one piece of wire to shape two branches, but not branches that directly oppose one another, as this won't work. Wind each wire as far along each branch as possible so that you don't have to use too many separate strands.

Remember!

○ Work outwards from the trunk; never inwards from the tip of the branch towards the trunk.

○ Keep your wiring neat. If you wish to coil a second wire onto a section of branch, always do so in the same direction as the first.

○ Avoid wires that cross, as this will make for pressure points which will scar the bark and spoil the appearance of the tree.

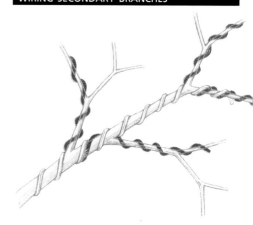

1 SECURE THE WIRE. THE PRINCIPLE WITH SECONDARY BRANCH WIRING IS TO SECURE WIRE BY COILING IT AROUND ANOTHER PRIMARY OR SECONDARY BRANCH WHICH IS ALREADY WIRED. YOU MAY NOW BE SURE THAT THE ENTIRE NETWORK OF BRANCHES IS A PART OF A 'WIRE SCULPTURE' WHOSE SECTIONS ARE CONNECTED, AND CAN BE MOVED INDEPENDENTLY. AS WITH PRIMARY BRANCHES, USE ONE STRAND OF WIRE FOR TWO NEARBY (BUT NOT OPPOSING) SECONDARY BRANCHES.

WIRING PRIMARY BRANCHES

1 SECURE THE WIRE. IT'S ALWAYS BEST TO WIRE TWO ADJACENT BRANCHES WITH ONE STRAND OF WIRE. START BY COILING THE WIRE AROUND THE TRUNK BETWEEN THE BRANCHES, THEN PASS IT UNDER THE BASE OF EACH BRANCH. FOR MAXIMUM EFFECT, THE SECTIONS OF WIRE ON THE TRUNK AND BRANCH SHOULD BOTH PASS IN THE SAME DIRECTION THROUGH THE FORK BETWEEN TRUNK AND BRANCH.

2 IF YOU CAN'T USE TWO BRANCHES, SECURE THE WIRE BY COILING IT AROUND THE TRUNK AT LEAST TWO FULL TURNS, ABOVE OR BELOW A BRANCH. AGAIN, THE WIRE ON THE TRUNK AND THAT ON THE BRANCH SHOULD PASS THROUGH THE FORK IN THE SAME DIRECTION. COIL THE WIRE ALONG THE BRANCH AS FAR AS POSSIBLE; IDEALLY, ALL THE WAY TO THE TIP. IF THE WIRE IS TOO THICK AND CLUMSY TO CONTINUE TO THE TIP OF THE BRANCH, STOP AND TREAT THE REMAINING SECTION AS IF IT WERE A SECONDARY BRANCH.

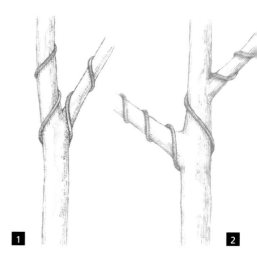

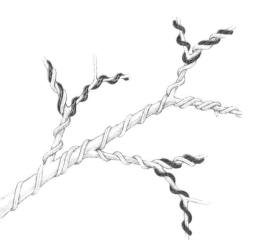

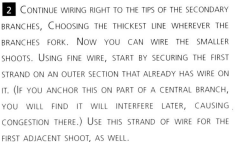

2 CONTINUE WIRING RIGHT TO THE TIPS OF THE SECONDARY BRANCHES, CHOOSING THE THICKEST LINE WHEREVER THE BRANCHES FORK. NOW YOU CAN WIRE THE SMALLER SHOOTS. USING FINE WIRE, START BY SECURING THE FIRST STRAND ON AN OUTER SECTION THAT ALREADY HAS WIRE ON IT. (IF YOU ANCHOR THIS ON PART OF A CENTRAL BRANCH, YOU WILL FIND IT WILL INTERFERE LATER, CAUSING CONGESTION THERE.) USE THIS STRAND OF WIRE FOR THE FIRST ADJACENT SHOOT, AS WELL.

3 NOW ANCHOR ANOTHER STRAND ONTO THE SHOOT YOU HAVE JUST WIRED. USE THIS STRAND FOR THE NEXT SHOOT ALONG. NO BRANCH WILL BE ENTIRELY CO-OPERATIVE AS FAR AS THE RELATIVE POSITIONS OF THE SECONDARY BRANCHES AND SHOOTS ARE CONCERNED. YOU WILL NEED TO BE IMAGINATIVE AND, DARE I SAY IT, CHEAT A LITTLE FROM TIME TO TIME. BUT IF YOU TRY YOUR LEVEL BEST TO FOLLOW THESE GUIDELINES, YOU WON'T GO TOO FAR WRONG.

ABOVE LEFT *Various thicknesses of wire have been used on different sized branches; tension wires are used to control the most stubborn branches.*
ABOVE RIGHT *All the wire you could wish for on display at a specialist bonsai nursery!*

REPOTTING

Taking the plunge

No plant can live happily for ever in the same pot. Eventually, it will become root bound; water will be unable to penetrate the soil, the roots find it impossible to grow any further, and the plant will die. Trees may need to be repotted because they require more space to grow in, or a new container may be chosen purely for aesthetic reasons. A handy rule of thumb is that young broadleaved trees require repotting every year; older trees need to be rehoused less frequently. Young conifers should be repotted every two years and older ones, perhaps every three to five years.

▸ MAKING SPACE FOR GROWTH ◂

Trees rely for survival on being able to produce new feeding roots annually, so one must provide this facility for bonsai. This does not mean that one needs to increase the size of the pot; space needs to be created within the existing pot. This is achieved by pruning the roots periodically, in late winter or early spring.

Pruning strikes fear in the heart of the bonsai novice, but once it becomes clear that the tree will thank you for it by growing with renewed vigour, it doesn't seem so radical!

If you forget to rehouse your bonsai for a year here and there, don't panic, just make sure that you remember to do it the following spring. As your tree develops and grows, you'll probably feel the need to change its container for one of a more appropriate shape or colour. It will be as well to have some guidance as to what is available.

Bonsai pots have three things in common

○ They are made of stoneware, which is fired at extremely high temperatures. This makes them frost-proof, so they will not flake or crack in freezing temperatures, as a pot made of earthenware might do.

○ They are not glazed on the inner surface. A slightly porous surface is more acceptable to roots than a glazed one.

○ Thirdly, and most importantly, they all have comparatively large drainage holes. Shallow pots drain more slowly than deep ones, and good drainage is vital. As a rough guide, a pot measuring 20x30cm (8x12in) should have two drainage holes, each at least 25mm (1in) in diameter. Some smart manufacturers even include a small extra hole in each corner through which to thread the wires should you need to bind the roots of the tree into the pot!

OPPOSITE *Simple containers and implements are employed in the practice of the complex and deeply satisfying art form that is bonsai.*

THE POTS FEATURED ON THE FOLLOWING PAGES ARE IDEALLY SUITED TO A RANGE OF BONSAI STYLES.

1 DEEP FLARED RECTANGLE

2 RECTANGULAR OR OVAL POT WITH LIP, SOFT CORNERS

3 SQUARE SECTION CASCADE POT

4 ROUND CASCADE POT

5 RECTANGLE WITHOUT LIP, HARD OR SQUARED CORNERS.

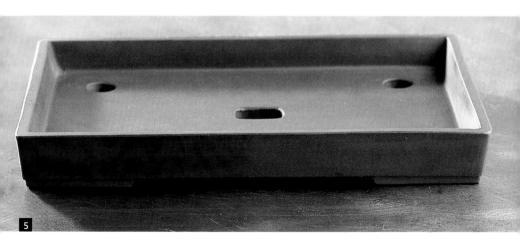

6 RUSTIC POT WITH A STONE FINISH

7 OVAL TRAY SUITABLE FOR GROUP PLANTINGS

8 FLARED ROUND POT

9 OVAL POT IN A NATURAL CLAY FINISH

10 ROUND TERRACOTTA DRUM

11 SELECTION OF *MAME* (TINY) POTS FOR MINIATURE TREES.

Watch point!
When choosing a container, make sure the base doesn't bow upward in the centre. This would cause water to collect in little pools in the corners. The roots of most bonsai trees hate being waterlogged.

▶ WHAT TYPE OF SOIL? ◀

Good soil for bonsai must be coarse and free-draining, to allow the roots to 'breathe' and prevent them from drowning. Provided the soil you use meets this requirement, and that you water and feed at appropriate intervals, your bonsai will survive. But there is a big difference between survival and thriving.

Plants can be grown in anything from pure sand to pure peat, but to stay in peak condition, bonsai trees need one of the generally accepted bonsai soils.

Akadama

This compressed volcanic clay is mined only in one small area of Japan. It is a pale orange-brown colour, and has one remarkable property. Unlike ordinary clays, it retains its granular structure when wet and takes a long time to break down into finer particles.

Akadama that is mined nearer the surface is generally soft, breaks down quickly, and cheaper. The best Akadama is mined at least 4m (13ft) below the ground. It is longer-lasting, harder and more expensive than other types.

In Japan, most conifers and virtually all deciduous bonsai are grown in Akadama soil.

This is now becoming standard practice in the West, with specialist bonsai nurseries in most countries holding stocks.

Akadama can be used neat or may be mixed with other ingredients such as grit and organic matter. Pines benefit from the addition of 30 per cent grit.

Kanuma

This is a soft mined soil from Japan. Pumice-based, it is used exclusively for Satsuki Azaleas as it has a low pH (it is acidic) which suits the azaleas as it retains moisture well. It crushes easily, so you need to take care not to compact it in the pot, which would turn it into dust.

Home-made soils

Many Western bonsai growers find it more practical (and more economical) to mix their own soils. This makes good sense because, with a bit of experimentation, it is possible to arrive at a recipe that suits one's own particular climate and watering schedule. If you are not able to water twice a day in summer, for example, your best option would be soil that retains more water, while if you live in a damp climate, you'll need a soil type that drains freely.

ABOVE *Akadama soil (1) is excellent for most trees; Kanuma soil (2) is ideal for azaleas; sifted peat (3) is often wasteful; horticultural grit (4) is essential for good drainage.*

Organic matter

Partially decayed organic matter is an excellent ingredient of soil, as it provides fertility, water retention and cation exchange capacity (CEC), which means that it can absorb nutrients and release them as the roots require them.

Organic matter also encourages the microbial activity essential to soil health. Peat is probably the best available type of organic matter, but it is a finite resource, and I agree with those who feel that its use is not environmentally friendly.

Leaf mould can be substituted for peat, but this quickly breaks down into dust. If you do use leaf mould, oak, pine and beech are the slowest to break down.

I find the sort of bark used by orchid growers to be the best all-round organic ingredient. It lasts for years and can be re-used. Also, when the bark is sifted, there is very little wastage.

Grit

Any good horticultural grit will do, provided it is lime-free. Beware of builders' sand, as it often contains impurities. Never use grit from the beach, because it is impregnated with salt, which will prove lethal to your bonsai.

Grit is essential to maintain an open soil structure and helps to provide good drainage.

Soil improvers

In recent years, a variety of products designed to be incorporated into soils have become available in nurseries and garden centres. These range from types of pumice to baked (calcined) clays.

Their advantage is that they are able to absorb a lot of of water without allowing soil to become waterlogged, and they maintain an open soil structure.

Although plants can be grown in pure pumice or clay, ideally their use should be restricted to a maximum of 20 per cent of a bonsai soil.

ABOVE *Composted orchid-grower's bark (5) is long-lasting, with little wastage; pumice (6) is a naturally occuring soil improver; calcined clay (7) can be sifted from old soil and reused.*

Preparing the ingredients for repotting can be hard work. First of all, you must sift out all the dust and fine particles – that is, anything smaller than 3mm (1/8in). Then, sift out all the oversized particles – those which are over 5 or 6mm (1/4in). When it comes to grit, 6mm particles are too large, so restrict them to about 4mm (3/16in) maximum size. Anything larger than this will inevitably seem like a boulder to any delicate bonsai!

Allow the mineral ingredients (the grit and improvers) to dry out completely. The organic ingredients must be dry, as a dry soil is easier to work with. However, take care that it does not become too dry, or it will repel moisture.

Basic recipe

This could not be simpler: it is merely a matter of combining 50 per cent organic matter and 50 per cent grit. Almost all species will be satisfied with this mixture. However, you can add up to 20 per cent of a soil improver if you like, and about the same proportion of Akadama. The compressed volcanic clay will make the soil feel more like ordinary garden soil but you will probably notice the difference more than your bonsai trees do.

The advantage of adding selected improvers and/or Akadama is that all of these additives will help the soil to maintain a free-draining, open structure as the organic matter breaks down in the fullness of time.

Variations

Some species will be even happier if the basic soil recipe is adjusted somewhat. For example, pines prefer a loose, free-draining soil, so the proportion of grit included in their soil mixture could be increased to as much as 60 or even 70 per cent. Japanese Maples, by contrast, greatly prefer their native Akadama, so you could either use that neat or increase the proportion that you usually add to your basic soil mixture.

Junipers are known to thrive on having a little fresh, chopped sphagnum moss included in the soil mix you use for them.

Flowering and fruiting bonsai trees and shrubs demand plenty of water, so it is a good idea to use a deep pot for these plants, and lavish plenty of organic matter on them.

ABOVE *Every keen gardener soon accumulates a collection of old pots and containers. These are ideal for growing bonsai in training until they are ready for their proper pots.*

▶ TAKING THE PLUNGE ◀

You have your pot and your soil ready. Now to get stuck in to repotting. Allow yourself plenty of time to enjoy the exercise. Have a spray bottle to hand, in order to keep the roots moist while you work. You'll also need sharp scissors, a root hook, a chopstick or knitting needle, wire and plastic mesh.

1 CHECK UNDERNEATH THE POT TO SEE IF THE TREE IS SECURED WITH WIRE. IF SO, CUT THESE WIRES WHERE THEY PASS THROUGH THE DRAINAGE HOLES. PUSH A BROAD-BLADED KNIFE (A PUTTY KNIFE WILL DO) BETWEEN SOIL AND POT USING A SAWING ACTION TO EASE THE ROOTS AWAY FROM THE POROUS WALLS OF THE POT. NOW, GENTLY EASE THE TREE FROM THE POT BY HOLDING THE TRUNK AT ITS BASE, AND TILTING ONE WAY AND THE OTHER. YOU MAY FEEL SOME RESISTANCE AS ROOTS ENTANGLED WITH THE DRAINAGE MESH BREAK. IF YOU INTEND TO USE THE SAME POT, KEEP THE EXPOSED ROOTS MOIST WHILE YOU WASH AND RINSE THE POT.

2 PREPARE THE POT BY FIXING SOME PLASTIC MESH OVER THE DRAINAGE HOLES. MAKE WIRE STAPLES WHICH YOU PUSH DOWN THROUGH THE MESH AND BEND OVER, UNDER THE POT.

TAKE TWO LENGTHS OF WIRE TO HOLD THE TREE IN THE POT. PUSH THE WIRES UP THROUGH THE HOLES PROVIDED, IF ANY. IF NOT, THREAD THE WIRES UP THROUGH THE MESH. BEND THEM OVER THE RIM OF THE POT.

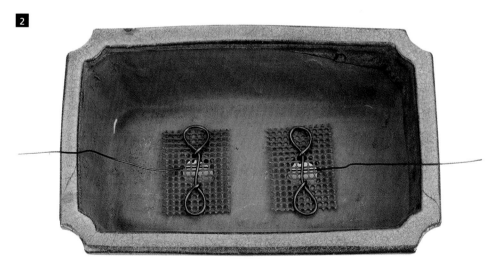

ABOVE *Drainage holes covered with mesh; and wires to secure the newly potted tree.*
TOP *The tightly packed root ball of a tree that is ready for repotting.*

3 Take your root hook or chopstick and begin to loosen the soil round the edges of the root mass (see right). Tease the roots out gently. You'll find that once you've loosened all round and underneath them, that the roots are not as dense towards the middle of the container.

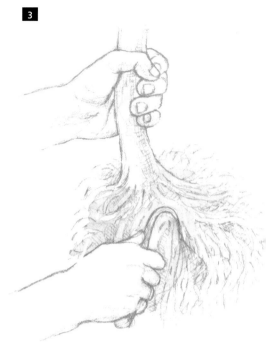

4 Rake the roots in a radial pattern, from the base of the trunk working outwards (below). Work deeper towards the outside of the root mass. Repeat this action on the underside of the root mass, too. Continue until you have removed half the total volume of soil, as shown below — more if it is compacted.

5 Now for the alarming bit: Comb the roots so that they hang down loosely (see opposite top) then, with very sharp scissors, cut all the thick roots right back as far as you can. This will encourage the growth of more fine, feeder roots.

6 Cut back the fine roots until the remaining root mass will fit comfortably into the pot with a clear margin allowed all round for new root growth.

8 PLACE A LAYER OF FRESH SOIL IN THE POT, NOT SO MUCH THAT THE TREE WILL BE RAISED HIGHER THAN IT WAS ORIGINALLY (UNLESS THAT IS YOUR INTENTION). MAKE A SMALL MOUND AT THE SPOT WHERE THE TRUNK WILL SIT. POSITION THE TREE IN THE POT AND TWIST IT GENTLY BACK AND FORTH TO SETTLE IT DOWN. THE MOUND OF SOIL CREATED WILL SPREAD AND WORK ITS WAY BETWEEN THE ROOTS BENEATH THE TRUNK. BRING THE WIRES OVER THE ROOT MASS AND TWIST THEM TOGETHER UNTIL THE TREE IS FIRMLY BEDDED AND DOESN'T ROCK AT ALL. THIS WILL PREVENT DELICATE NEW ROOTS FROM BEING DAMAGED AS THE TREE IS MOVED OR IF IT IS EXPOSED TO STRONG WIND.

9 ADD MORE SOIL AND WORK IT BETWEEN THE ROOTS WITH THE CHOPSTICK. DON'T POKE IT, PUSH THE STICK INTO THE SOIL AND MOVE IT WITH A CIRCULAR MOTION, JUST AS IF YOU WERE STIRRING COFFEE. PAY ATTENTION TO THIS PART OF THE OPERATION, BECAUSE IF THERE ARE ANY EMPTY SPACES, THE ROOTS IN THE AFFECTED AREA WON'T BE ABLE TO FUNCTION PROPERLY. CONTINUE TO ADD SOIL, WORKING IT BETWEEN THE ROOTS UNTIL THE POT IS FILLED. LEVEL THE SOIL OFF BUT DON'T PRESS IT DOWN, OR IT MAY BECOME COMPACTED WHICH WILL DAMAGE THE ROOTS. TRY TO AVOID MOUNDING SOIL UP AROUND THE TRUNK, AS THE *NEBARI* SHOULD BE EVIDENT. LEAVE THE SOIL ABOUT 6MM (1/4IN) BELOW THE RIM OF THE POT. THIS WILL HELP LATER ON WHEN IT BECOMES DENSE AND

7 THE WIDTH OF THIS MARGIN WILL DEPEND ON THE SIZE OF THE ROOT MASS, AND OF THE POT. AS A RULE OF THUMB, A 200x300MM (8x12IN) POT SHOULD HAVE A CLEAR MARGIN OF ABOUT 25MM (1IN). SPRAY THE ROOTS AGAIN TO KEEP THE CUT ENDS MOIST.

8

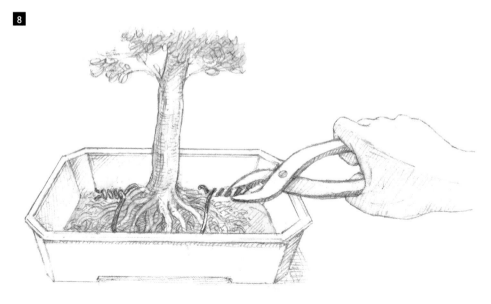

9

MATTED WITH NEW ROOTS. ALSO, THE WATER MAY TAKE A FEW MOMENTS TO SOAK IN, AND IF THE SOIL IS LEVEL WITH THE POT RIM, THE SURPLUS WILL JUST RUN OFF INSTEAD OF BEING ABSORBED INTO THE SOIL.

10 FINALLY, GIVE THE PLANT ENOUGH WATER TO MOISTEN IT THOROUGHLY. ALLOW THE POT TO DRAIN FOR A FEW MINUTES, AND WATER AGAIN. KEEP THE TREE AWAY FROM FROST, RAIN AND WIND UNTIL IT HAS RE-ESTABLISHED ITSELF AND STARTED TO GROW AGAIN. DON'T FEED IT AT ALL FOR THREE WEEKS. CHECK OFTEN THAT THE SOIL HASN'T BECOME DRY, BUT IT IS MOST IMPORTANT THAT YOU DO NOT OVER WATER THE REPOTTED PLANT AT THIS CRUCIAL STAGE.

10

GROWING YOUR OWN
BONSAI
Creating a unique work of art

The true joy of bonsai is growing your own from seeds, cuttings, garden plants or wild trees. It's a slow process but whether it takes you five years or 25, your reward will be the living work of art that you have created.

▶ SUITABLE SPECIES ◀

In deciding which species to try, there are several points to consider. The plant you choose:

○ should have naturally small leaves. Leaves will become smaller with bonsai training, but there is a limit to how much they can be reduced. This applies to broadleaved trees, conifers, tropicals and hardy species.

○ should be of a species able to survive indefinitely in a container. A tree at the nursery may live happily in a pot but will it continue to do so for the next 100 years? For example, not all species are able to tolerate root pruning. Others demand a free run of roots as they mature. The staff at the garden centre or nursery may guide your choice. Say what you want the plant for, and they will probably be intrigued and happy to help.

○ should have branches flexible enough to train with wires. (Do not snap twigs off the nursery's stock, but a gentle tweak here and there will do no harm!)

○ should respond well to pruning by throwing out new buds on old wood, as well as at the site of the cut. Here, the local nursery staff may not be as helpful, as many species that oblige in this way are not pruned in garden cultivation, so they wouldn't have much idea. As a guide, look at the interior of the plant. If you see buds or young shoots, the chances are good that it will respond well to pruning. Any species used for hedges could be developed into a bonsai winner; as might those used for topiary, or any which regularly feature in arrangements, either as foliage or flowers.

○ should be a species for which you can provide the appropriate conditions. Take your local climate into account. For example, don't buy a hardy pine, which craves very cold conditions, if you can't leave it outside in the winter. If your home is cool with a dry atmosphere, tropical species will not enjoy living with you unless they have their own artificial micro-environment.

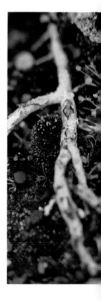

OPPOSITE *A handsome driftwood San Jose Juniper, trained in the Semi-Cascade Style.*

▶ USING LOCAL SPECIES ◀

The only reason that most masterpiece bonsai are created from Japanese or Chinese species is because that is where bonsai has been practised for generations, and masterpiece bonsai really do take generations to perfect. The majority of commercial bonsai are also oriental species simply because most of them are produced in the East. But this does not mean that Orientals hold the monopoly on species good for bonsai. Far from it!

In Europe, stately Scots Pines possess unique qualities that make them a joy to work with. Not only are they a wonderful colour, but they perform most obligingly.

The Sabina Junipers of southern Europe are just as good as the Japanese Shimpaku, with their swirling natural sharis and fine, rich foliage.

The robust San Jose and Californian Junipers of the USA form impressively strong, sturdy bonsai, and Swamp Cypresses have trunks that any Japanese bonsai grower would drool over!

In Canada, larches and Pencil Cedars have the capacity to look ancient, even when they are quite

ABOVE *Native to America, the American Larch* (Larix laricini) *makes an interesting bonsai as it manages to appear aged and battered in a very short space of time.*
TOP *This striking wispy bonsai tree is a Scots Pine* (Pinus sylvestris) *in the Windswept or Fukinagashi Style.*

young, and they produce fairly dense foliage after just a couple of years.

The wild olives of southern Africa provide their bonsai artists with opportunities to produce powerful images in a perfect growing climate. This is a source of envy to those of us who are not able to indulge our passion all year round. Australians, meanwhile, are creating vigorous, resilient miniature Port Jackson Figs that are every bit as good as any tropical bonsai produced in the East. Heavy trunks and branches are built rapidly, and the figs' stubby twigs bear masses of buds, producing small, dense leaves.

Look around you, study the trees that grow in your part of the world. Analyze their structures and try to visualize them as bonsai. What you will see is the golden future of bonsai as a truly global art form.

ABOVE LEFT *A bonsai created from a South African Veld Fig* (Ficus Burtt-Davyi), *which is both drought resistant and frost tolerant.*
ABOVE RIGHT *A larch* (Larix spp.) *in early spring. This is in the Literati or Bunjin Style, developed by Chinese bonsai practitioners a long time ago.*

▶ BONSAI FROM YOUNGER PLANTS ◀

Propagation

From seeds If you're a novice bonsai grower, don't sow seeds for your first attempt. It will be four or five years before you can actually do anything meaningful with them. Having said that, everyone should grow at least some bonsai from seed because there's no better way to learn about the mechanics of plant growth. The venerable Japanese master, Kyuzo Murata, was still growing trees from seed up to his death, when he was in his late eighties! Another good reason to grow from seed is to feed your passion for a species that is not available to you in any other form.

Seeds of native species are available and just waiting to be collected from trees that occur naturally in your area. Wait until the fruits are ripe and the tree has begun to shed them. Choose the plumpest, healthiest-looking fruits and pick them, rather than gathering fallen ones.

Exotic species are more difficult to acquire. Check out the small advertisements in gardening magazines and send off for seed catalogues. Winter is the best time to do this, because you can be reasonably sure that the seeds will arrive in plenty of time for sowing.

Good seed merchants will offer detailed sowing instructions along with the seeds of your chosen species. Some seeds, such as the hard-shelled seeds of hardy species, need a period of subzero temperatures (stratification) before they are able to germinate. Others, like the eucalyptus, are stimulated to germinate by searing heat. Many seeds, especially large ones collected by squirrels in autumn and buried for future use, should be sown straight after collection; as is nature's way.

If you collect seeds you won't have instructions, so allow nature to take its course. There are tricks to encourage germination, but simply sow them outside when you get them.

ABOVE *Commercial nurseries propagate cuttings in vast quantities, from which many fledgling plants will eventually become bonsai for beginners.*

Seeds normally distributed by the wind should be settled on the soil surface and sprinkled with sand to hold them in place. Larger, wind-distributed seeds can be pushed into the soil with their wings left exposed.

Hard seeds from berries should be pressed firmly into the soil. (These may take up to two years to germinate because the tough shells have to disintegrate first.) Very large seeds should be buried to a depth roughly equal to twice their size. Then, just ensure that the soil stays damp and wait.

Aftercare Newly germinated seeds are vulnerable to 'damping-off', the term for a variety of fungal diseases that cause the stems to collapse. Spray with copper-based fungicide every two weeks as a preventive measure.

As soon as the first two or three leaves appear, lift the seedlings one by one, by pushing a stick underneath them and prising them up. (Always handle seedlings by the leaves and not by tender stems.) Repot them in individual pots, spreading the roots out as far as they will go. This will provide you with good *nebari* (surface roots) in the future.

Keep the seedlings in the shade until they have produced a few sets of true leaves. Then introduce them gradually to full light, at which point you can begin to feed sparingly.

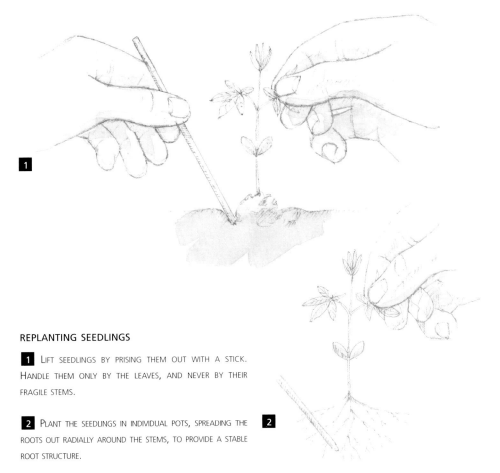

REPLANTING SEEDLINGS

1 LIFT SEEDLINGS BY PRISING THEM OUT WITH A STICK. HANDLE THEM ONLY BY THE LEAVES, AND NEVER BY THEIR FRAGILE STEMS.

2 PLANT THE SEEDLINGS IN INDIVIDUAL POTS, SPREADING THE ROOTS OUT RADIALLY AROUND THE STEMS, TO PROVIDE A STABLE ROOT STRUCTURE.

Cuttings

Many, but not all, species root easily from cuttings. Books on propagation provide lists, so check in your local library.

Softwood and semi-ripe cuttings These are taken from growing shoots before they get woody. Softwood cuttings are infant shoots; semi-ripe cuttings are those taken as the shoots begin to change colour.

Hardwood cuttings From shoots that have gone woody. The current year's growth can be taken in autumn, but older shoots will do, too. Allow them to grow for a year before potting up individually. Hardwood cuttings root best in the open ground, but they can also be rooted in deep pots.

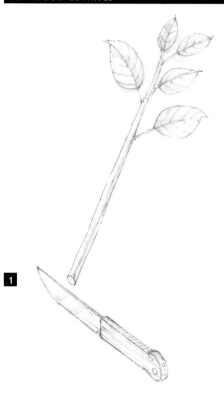

1 CUT THROUGH THE SHOOT WITH A SHARP KNIFE, JUST BELOW AN INTERNODE. CUT OFF MOST OF THE LOWER LEAVES, LEAVING AT LEAST TWO OR THREE AT THE TOP.

2 DIP THE END IN HORMONE ROOTING POWDER AND INSERT THE CUTTING IN A WELL-DRAINED POT OR IN A TRAY OF SANDY SOIL. INSERT THE CUTTING UP TO ABOUT HALF ITS LENGTH. MOISTEN WELL, AND INCLUDE SOME COPPER FUNGICIDE IN THE WATER.

3 USE A PROPAGATOR WITH A LID, IF YOU HAVE ONE. IF NOT, MAKE A PLASTIC 'TENT' SUPPORTED BY A WIRE FRAME. DO NOT ALLOW ANY LEAVES TO TOUCH THE PROPAGATOR LID OR THE PLASTIC TENT, BECAUSE THIS INVARIABLY LEADS TO FUNGAL INFECTION OF THE SHOOT.

ABOVE *Young, rooted cuttings growing happily in individual containers. Most plants respond well to being grown from cuttings.*

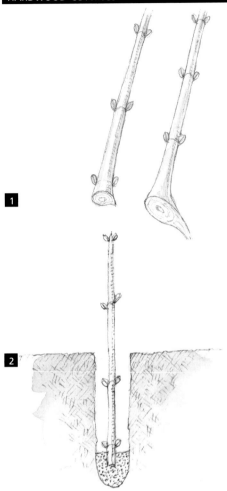

1 PULL AWAY AN ENTIRE SHOOT WITH A 'HEEL' OF THE PREVIOUS YEAR'S GROWTH ATTACHED, OR CUT JUST BELOW AN INTERNODE. USE A SHARP KNIFE TO TRIM AWAY LOOSE BARK AROUND THE HEEL CUTTINGS.

2 USE A STICK TO MAKE A HOLE IN FREE-DRAINING SOIL AND SPRINKLE SOME SAND IN THE BOTTOM. SETTLE THE CUTTING GENTLY IN THE SAND AND LOOSELY REFILL THE HOLE. THERE'S NO NEED TO WORRY ABOUT ANY AFTERCARE, AND NATURE CAN TAKE ITS COURSE. ONCE THE CUTTING HAS ESTABLISHED ITSELF IT CAN BE POTTED UP.

Layering

This is my favourite method of propagating bonsai material. It enables you to obtain a plant with mature characteristics in just a few months. Layering is rather like a giant cutting, but it offers the considerable advantage that you don't separate the new plant from the parent tree until it has more than sufficient roots of its own to survive independently.

In general, any species which roots easily from a cutting, will also do so by layering. Plants that are reluctant to root from cuttings have a much higher success rate when layered. However, some stubborn species make no effort to strike roots at all – most pines fall into this category. Nevertheless, there's nothing to lose by having a go.

First, find a suitable branch, anything over 1cm (3/8in) thick. Choose one with an interesting shape and bark texture as well as some handy sub-branches. You can begin wire training these before, or during, the layering process. The best time for this is late spring and early summer, while the tree is growing vigorously. (Left too late in the year, there may not be time for new roots to become established before winter sets in and the potential layer will be doomed to failure – though this is less of a problem in temperate areas.)

You'll need a sharp knife, some strong plastic (freezer bags will do), some string and some fresh sphagnum moss. If you don't have moss, you can use peat or even a seed compost but moss gives the best results. It also holds the new roots together firmly when you come to sever the layer from the parent tree. You will find that other rooting mediums tend to fall away, often taking the new roots with them!

The time taken for roots to develop varies tremendously between species. Azaleas can take three years, but elms, maples, junipers and most tropicals will root within a couple of months and can be severed in the coming autumn.

Aftercare

Having severed your layer from the parent tree, plant it in an ample pot. Use ordinary bonsai soil, and water well. Protect the layer against extreme temperature changes until the following spring. The roots are young and delicate and stress may kill them. In a cold climate, a shady greenhouse or polythene tunnel offers the best environment. Shade and regular misting helps in warmer areas. Allow the layers to grow for a year before further training. At the next repotting, the moss can be raked from the roots and the stub of the original branch can be cut out.

ABOVE *Some branches on old trees may bow so low that they make contact with the earth and begin to take root.*

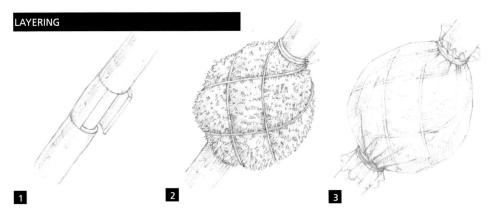

1

2

3

1 DECIDE WHERE NEW ROOTS SHOULD FORM AND CUT THROUGH THE BARK AT THIS POINT. CUT THROUGH TO WOOD ALL ROUND THE BRANCH. MAKE A SECOND CUT BELOW THE FIRST. THE DISTANCE BETWEEN THESE SHOULD BE 1.5 TIMES THE THICKNESS OF THE BRANCH. PEEL BARK AWAY BETWEEN THE CUTS. SCRAPE ANY CAMBIUM FROM THE EXPOSED WOOD. (CAMBIUM WILL BRIDGE THE GAP SO THE LAYER WON'T WORK.)

2 SOAK THE SPHAGNUM MOSS AND GENTLY SQUEEZE OUT THE EXCESS WATER. WRAP A WAD OF THE MOSS AROUND THE DEBARKED AREA, MAKING SURE THAT THE 2.5CM (1IN) ABOVE IT IS ADEQUATELY COVERED. THE BALL OF MOSS SHOULD BE ABOUT THE SIZE OF A TENNIS BALL. WITH ANY BRANCHES OVER 4CM (1.5 IN) THICK THE AMOUNT OF MOSS SHOULD BE INCREASED. TIE THE SPHAGNUM MOSS LOOSELY INTO PLACE.

3 NOW WRAP THE CLEAR PLASTIC AROUND THE MOSS, SECURING IT BOTH ABOVE AND BELOW WITH STRING. TIE IT TIGHTLY ENOUGH SO THE MOSS WON'T SLIP BUT NOT SO FIRMLY AS TO RESTRICT THE FREE FLOW OF SAP. DON'T WORRY ABOUT THE MOSS DRYING OUT: AS THE NEW ROOTS TAKE IN MOISTURE, THE XYLEM REMAINS ACTIVE, AND WILL BE CONTINUALLY PUMPING WATER INTO THE MOSS!

4 WHITE (OR RED) ROOT TIPS WILL APPEAR BETWEEN THE MOSS AND THE PLASTIC WRAP. DON'T ACT TOO SOON. IF THE TIPS ARE WHITE, THEY ARE TOO STILL TOO TENDER TO DISTURB. WAIT UNTIL THEY TURN BROWN, THEN CUT OFF THE LAYER BELOW THE PLASTIC. UNTIE THE STRING, PEELING AWAY THE PLASTIC AND TAKING CARE NOT TO INTERFERE WITH THE MOSS OR ROOTS. DON'T TRY TO SHORTEN THE STUB OF THE ORIGINAL BRANCH AT THIS STAGE. IT WILL HELP TO STABILIZE THE NEW PLANT IN ITS POT.

5 PLANT THE LAYER WITH THE BALL OF MOSS IN AN AMPLE, DEEP POT, MAKING SURE THE MOSS IS COVERED WITH SOIL. SECURE THE LAYER IN THE POT BY PASSING A LENGTH OF STRING BETWEEN SOME CONVENIENT BRANCHES AND THE TRUNK, AND TYING IT AROUND THE POT. WATER WELL AND PLACE IN A SHELTERED POSITION.

4

5

▸ TRAINING A YOUNG BONSAI ◂

Developing bonsai from seedlings or cuttings allows you total control over every aspect of its final form: size, style, and shape. However, if you want a large bonsai, it can be a long process. With layers, you already have an established trunk and the makings of the branches, which will save you years. On the other hand, you will never be able to change the shape of the trunk, so the original choice of a branch for layering is important.

When to start

You can begin training as soon as the young plant has become settled into its container – usually after one growing season. If the trunk is flexible, wire it (see p100) and introduce the shape you have chosen. Make sure that there is a viable bud or shoot on the outside of each curve from which the branches will be built. Also, don't forget to make bends to the back and front, as well as from side to side. Bend the top of the tree towards the front a little, to add depth to the perspective.

If the trunk is too stiff to bend without causing damage, prune it above a bud where you want the first branch to grow. The shoot can later be wired upward to form a new leader. After this has been pruned, more shoots will grow from the first cut, and one of these can be trained as the first branch. Continue this process until the desired height and number of branches has been achieved. You'll probably find that you employ a combination of these techniques as the tree develops. Be sure to remove wires before they scar the bark!

While this process is taking place, the tree will grow and develop much faster if it's in a large container, or in the open ground. A tree in open ground is able to achieve a 5cm (2 in) thick trunk within three or four years – in a small pot this could take a lifetime.

TRAINING CUTTINGS AND SEEDLINGS

1 If the stem is flexible you can shape it with wire, making sure there is a bud or shoot on the outside of each curve. Cut the top off the stem below the level that you have decided will be the ultimate height of the tree. You may wire the bases of the main branches into position at the same time or decide to grow a new set from scratch.

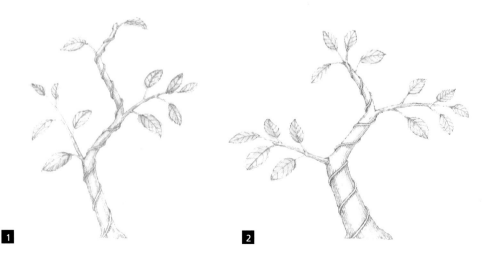

1

2

2 RIGID STEMS SHOULD BE CUT BACK TO A CONVENIENT INTERNODE. TRAIN ONE NEW SHOOT AS THE FIRST BRANCH, AND ANOTHER AS A NEW LEADER. REPEAT THIS PATTERN UNTIL THE TRUNK IS ALMOST AS TALL AS YOU WISH THE FINAL HEIGHT OF THE TREE TO BE. TRAIN THE FIRST SECTION OF THE BRANCHES AS YOU DEVELOP THE TRUNK.

3 ALLOW LOWER BRANCHES TO GROW MORE STRONGLY THAN THE UPPER BRANCHES AND THE LEADER. THIS WILL CAUSE THE LOWER PART OF THE TRUNK TO THICKEN, AND CREATE THE ALL-IMPORTANT TAPER. KEEP THE APEX WEAK BY REMOVING VIGOROUS SHOOTS AND THINNING OUT DENSE AREAS AS THEY DEVELOP. YOU WILL PROBABLY HAVE TO CUT OUT THE ENTIRE APEX AND REBUILD IT AT LEAST ONCE, DURING THE PROTRACTED DEVELOPMENT PROCESS.

4 ONCE THE BRANCHES HAVE THICKENED, CUT THEM ALL BACK TO THE FIRST INTERNODE. THIS WILL STIMULATE NEW SHOOTS WHICH SHOULD BE TRAINED WITH WIRE AND THEN ALLOWED TO GROW FREELY FOR A SEASON OR TWO. THEY, TOO, MUST THEN BE CUT BACK TO THE FIRST OR SECOND INTERNODES, AND THE WHOLE PROCESS REPEATED. ALLOW ONE OR TWO SHOOTS TO THE REAR OF THE LOWER BRANCHES TO REMAIN UNPRUNED, SO THAT THEY WILL GO ON DRAWING ENERGY TO THICKEN THE LOWER TRUNK. THESE CAN BE CUT OFF LATER ON, WHEN THEY HAVE COMPLETED THEIR IMPORTANT TASK.

Redirecting the energy

Trees are naturally apically dominant (they want to grow upward as fast as possible). This urge has to be controlled, and the energy redirected to the lower branches, otherwise they will become weak and may eventually die.

You will also want to create exaggerated taper from the roots to the top of the trunk, which is achieved by directing energy into the lower branches. If the lower branches carry a very heavy burden of foliage, they will thicken up and the trunk below them will follow suit.

To redirect the energy, keep the growth in the upper part of the tree thinned out. Cut away vigorous shoots at their bases, leaving the more fragile ones in place. Now and again it will probably be necessary to cut away the top section entirely, in order to rebuild it.

Allow a little more vigour in the next tier of branches and more still in the tier below that, and so on. The lowest branches should be permitted to grow unhindered as far as possible. As a result of this practice, your developing bonsai might well be three or four times as wide as it is high after a few years, but this is just a temporary stage.

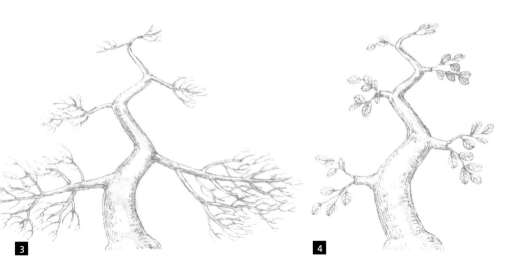

After a couple of years, all the branches may be cut back to the first internode, to encourage forks close to the trunk. The shoots that develop following this operation should then also be treated in the same way as the first generation of shoots but for a shorter period of time. They should, too, be pruned a little more frequently, to encourage much greater ramification.

Wiring can be done whenever it is necessary or convenient. But remember that the tree is growing fast, so branches won't take very long to set and wires must be removed before they damage the bark.

On the lower branches, it is a good idea to allow one or two 'sacrificial' secondary branches to remain unpruned for a few seasons. These should be positioned close to the trunk and towards the rear of the tree. The sacrificed branches will act as pumps, and will draw energy into the lower branches. This will thicken the bases of the branches; as well as further enhancing the taper of the trunk.

You can leave branches to bolt at the back of the trunk but if you do this, make sure that you have chosen the correct front elevation. Only when you have built a good, solid trunk and established a basic framework of branches should you consider planting the tree in a bonsai pot. It is amazing how much the confinement of a tree to a shalllow container will slow down its rate of growth.

ABOVE *A few of the development beds at the Hong Kong Artistic Pot Plant Association.*

▸ BONSAI FROM LARGER PLANTS ◂

Most enthusiasts prefer to create their bonsai by reducing the size of larger trees which already have mature bark and impressive nebari, as well as thicker trunks. This way, images of majestic, mature trees can be created in a comparatively short time. The only drawback is that shortening a 3m (10ft) trunk, inevitably leaves a large wound which will be evident for many decades. This wound must be either hidden at the back of the tree, or incorporated into the design.

The best start you can make is to choose the right material. So, which desirable physical characteristics should you seek?

Nursery plants

In the case of small plants that you intend to enlarge, almost all physical characteristics can either be easily altered, or will change naturally as the tree matures. In larger plants, the roots, the trunk, and even some of the branches, will be too thick and rigid to consider bending. You can see, therefore, that the initial choice of material is crucial to your success.

Although the nebari are important, you should begin by examining the shape and character of the lower trunk. An upright, cylindrical trunk with little natural taper will always look boring. Ideal trunks should demonstrate movement as they leave the soil,

TOP Garden nurseries are frequently able to offer treasure troves of superb potential bonsai material to those with the experience to know what to look out for.

ABOVE *Take time to examine the nebari before making your final decision. If you cannot see excellent nebari immediately, choose another plant.*

and should have healthy lower branches. Once you've found a few suitable specimens check their nebari.

Less-than-perfect exposed roots can be disguised by altering the planting angle of the trunk, so take time to select the best specimen. A good trunk with superb nebari makes a better bonsai than one with poor nebari.

If you are still undecided, examine the existing branches. Bear in mind that on conifers (particularly pines) you won't easily be able to regenerate new foliage close to the trunk. By contrast, with broadleaved species you could take off all the branches and re-grow them from scratch!

Don't try to design a tree on the spot; it will evolve when all the options have been considered. However, do try to visualize its eventual size and style. Imagine how existing branches might be shortened and incorporated into the design.

What to avoid

It's all too easy to be carried away by the sight of beautiful spring flowers on an ornamental cherry or stunning autumn tints on a red-leafed maple. But beware, many ornamental varieties are grafted onto the rootstocks of parent species, or onto dwarfing rootstock.

The pressures of commercial production mean that these are often cleft, or crown grafts, and can leave ugly scars. Dwarfing rootstock can cause trunks to taper downward instead of upward. An invigorating rootstock can result in ugly swellings at the union. You may overlook such failings, but in time may regret hasty decisions.

Avoid sickly bargain-basement plants, it is no bargain if it succumbs! Don't buy plants if the nebari can't be seen, even by scraping away soil around the trunk. When saplings are potted up for sale, the roots are often pushed to the bottom of the pot and covered with earth, What looks like an interesting short trunk might hide an ugly, straight section, buried in the pot. Know what you're getting before you buy!

ABOVE *Many ornamental varieties are grafted low on trunks. Their unions may be poorly executed, causing swellings and scars which will never improve.*

▶ COLLECTING PLANTS FROM OPEN GROUND ◀

The advantage of collecting material from the open ground is that it will often look old and can demonstrate characteristics which offer exciting possibilities. Most home gardens and vacant plots contain shrubs and small trees that are perfect for bonsai, and which are often overlooked.

Fertile growing conditions, plus regular clipping and care, produce the type of dense, healthy plants that are crying out to be potted up and converted to beautiful bonsai. Gardens frequently offer a range of species not easily found in the wild or in nurseries, such as dwarf conifers, flowering shrubs, even culinary herbs.

Keep an eye out for garden reconstructions, or for neighbours who complain of shrubs and trees that have outgrown their allotted space.

If you are lucky enough to have suitable plants growing in your own garden (and a suitably sympathetic spouse), you can start the training by hard-pruning and wiring while the plant is still in the ground. At this stage it will benefit from an extensive root system, which makes both regeneration and development much faster than would be possible in a container.

Much prize bonsai material is to be found in the wild. In mountainous areas, exposure to harsh conditions has a stunting effect, while in lowland meadows, deer or horses browse on many species, producing hummocks of dense foliage. Bear in mind, though, that wild

ABOVE *Road construction schemes threaten both urban and wilderness areas. Collecting trees from sites like these will save them from certain death.*

plants are not our property, they form part of a natural environment which we hold in trust for future generations. The greed and carelessness of hordes of collectors has had a devastating effect on flora.

Most nations have stringent environmental protection legislation, which prohibits or restricts collection of certain species from the wild. Some countries forbid the taking of any indigenous plants. Such laws are in place to protect the environment and must be respected and obeyed.

Legitimate collection is a possibility in the wild, however. A tract of land may be owned by a farmer or a forestry company. If so,

contact the owner, explain why you would like a particular plant and ask for permission to take it. As often as not, you will get the go-ahead. Watch out for land clearance operations, road building, quarrying, or anything that suggests that an area containing the right sort of material is about to fall prey to a team of bulldozers.

Lowland areas, where animals browse or farmers repeatedly cut plants back, can be veritable goldmines of bonsai-in-the-making. Look carefully along roadsides, field margins, wasteland, and even in neglected suburban gardens. Always remember to seek permission before you start digging operations.

TOP Areas of wilderness, like this rocky outcrop, can provide one with a wealth of superb bonsai material. However, digging is difficult and almost always illegal. Do seek permission before collecting any plants from the wild.

What to look for

The same desirable features are shared by wild and nursery plants, but you need to be open-minded about what to look for in the wild.

You are not going to find a perfect, ready-made bonsai. What you may find, however, is a plant with unique characteristics of the sort that could never be successfully imitated by human intervention. Features to look out for include hollow, old wounds, thick, cracked bark, and grotesquely contorted trunks and branches on which sharis have been etched by the elements.

A plant in the wild may actually be no more than 20 or 30 years old, but it might display all the characteristics of a tree many times its age. Don't be misled into assuming that a low dome of dense foliage conceals a bonsai gem; more often than not, the trunks and branches are either uninspiring or inappropriate.

Take the time to examine each tree carefully; don't dig up the first one you stumble across. There's not much point in labouring over an unsuitable wild tree, just to avoid going home empty-handed from a field trip.

Be vigilant when checking the nebari. The stems of many wild seedlings travel along the ground beneath the grasses before finding their way up towards the light. Or, an otherwise tasty piece of material, with what looks like a short, stout trunk, may have an irritating long section concealed beneath the undergrowth. Check on this before you dig.

It's understandable that the first flush of excitement at finding a wonderful piece of material should make you want to whip it right out of the ground.

However, as with every other aspect of bonsai, patience is a virtue. It makes no sense to collect a plant out of season, or in a rush before the sun sets, only to spend the following months attending at its deathbed! It is far better to take home one plant with a good chance of survival, than a carload of potential corpses.

Paying attention to the rules (see below) and putting them into practice, should offer you and your precious tree the best chance of a long and mutually rewarding relationship.

Digging plants from the ground

To start with:
- Don't collect the first plant you find.
- Don't collect out of season. Plants always transplant better in late winter or early spring, before their buds open. Some can be collected in high summer but only resort to doing this if you know it will work.
- Don't even think of yanking plants out of the ground with your bare hands because you don't have the right tools with you.
- Don't leave bare roots exposed to air for longer than is absolutely necessary.
- Don't collect more plants than you need, or than you can pot immediately you get home.
- Finally, never collect from the wild without first gaining permission.

Do:
- Hunt for plants in summer and come back in late winter, prepared for collection.
- Take with you all the equipment that you may require: digging tools, root-saw, string, plastic sheeting and secateurs.
- Take your time. Keep as many roots as possible undisturbed, by gathering a large rootball. (Some specialized techniques involve taking two seasons to collect a plant.)
- Keep the roots moist and the rootball intact until you get it home.
- Pot up the plant immediately on your return, using a previously prepared container filled with the appropriate type of soil.
- Always leave the site of your collection tidy. Go to some trouble to refill the hole neatly, restore any vegetation that you may have disturbed by your digging operation and clean up and carry away all debris.

Aftercare

Digging the plant out is only half the operation. Now to ensure its survival. On the way home, protect the root ball from heat and cold. Once there, plant your acquisition in an oversized container – wooden boxes with slatted bases, covered with mesh, offer good drainage. Prepare some very open soil. Standard bonsai soil (see p110) with extra grit will suit your new acquisition very well indeed.

Unpack the root ball carefully, cutting away the plastic with a sharp knife. Allow any loose earth to fall away. Use a root hook or chopstick to gently loosen the soil, then rinse off the remaining soil, using a hose. There's no need to remove all the soil at this stage, but exposing the ends of the cut roots encourages the development of new ones. Tie the tree firmly into the container before you begin filling in with soil. Add more soil slowly, working it in between the roots, leaving no empty pockets. Take time, this is important.

Then, water thoroughly, place the tree in a sheltered spot (perhaps in an open-ended polythene tunnel) and keep it moist, spraying the foliage frequently. Don't feed the plant at all until growth is properly established.

Collected plants require two years to recover from the trauma of relocation before being exposed to further training. But in the summer months, a light trim is permissible.

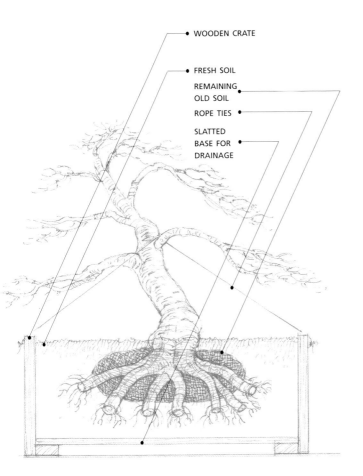

WOODEN CRATE

FRESH SOIL

REMAINING OLD SOIL

ROPE TIES

SLATTED BASE FOR DRAINAGE

HOUSING A NEWLY COLLECTED BONSAI

USE A HOSE TO WASH AWAY SOME OF THE OUTER SOIL. THIS IS KINDER TO DELICATE ROOTS THAN RAKING EARTH AWAY WITH A HOOK. THE NEWLY COLLECTED TREE SHOULD BE FIRMLY TIED INTO A LARGE CONTAINER (PREFERABLY A WOODEN ONE) WHICH ALLOWS AMPLE ROOM FOR THE NEW ROOTS TO SPREAD THEMSELVES OUT. MAKE SURE ALL THE ROOTS ARE WELL-COVERED WITH FRESH SOIL.

▸ THE DIG ◂

Before you start digging, cut back all overlong branches so that you can work close to the trunk. Cutting back long branches will also reduce demands on the sparse roots that are left to the plant after collection. (Remember that if you remove foliage from a conifer branch, the branch will die, while with a broadleaved tree it's possible to cut back hard.)

Start excavation by removing the surface vegetation and rocks around the base of the trunk. Next, scrape away some soil to establish where the heavy roots emerge from the trunk. Dig a circular trench round the plant. Make the

circle as wide as possible, at least 60cm (2ft) across. Work slowly and methodically, taking care not to damage the fine roots. Cut through thick roots cleanly with a saw and remove one section of the root so that you can continue excavating.

Once you have dug below the level of the radiating roots, it is necessary to start undercutting the root ball. (Somewhere underneath the trunk will be one or two thick, deep roots, so allow yourself ample time and space to work in.) As you mine under the root ball, gently rock the plant, this will give some

TOP Even dwarf conifers eventually outgrow their allotted space. They can be easily lifted to begin a new life as bonsai.

indication as to where the remaining large roots are located. Find these heavy roots and cut them with a saw. To do this, you might have to lie flat in the mud!

Having severed the last roots, lift the root ball out of the hole, without shaking off all the soil. To do this, tilt the root ball to one side, as far as it will go; and slide a sheet of heavy plastic underneath it. Roll up the side of the plastic sheet that is tucked under the roots, so that when you tilt the root ball in the opposite direction, the sheet can be unrolled and the roots will be in the centre of the plastic.

The roots must be kept moist, so have a spray bottle of water to hand. Wrapping the roots in damp sphagnum moss will help (if you are lucky, some will be available at the site). Now draw the plastic sheet tightly around the root ball. Fix the sheet firmly into place with string or strong adhesive packing tape. Be lavish with the tape, the roots must not be disturbed at all when you move the plant.

Lift out the root ball if it isn't heavy. If it is, dig a ramp and roll it out gently. Handle the plant by the root ball, not the trunk, to avoid damaging young roots growing from its base.

ABOVE *Junipers were once commonplace in the mountains of Japan, but they are now rare. Consequently, bonsai created from them command high prices.*

OBTAINING A NEW PLANT FROM A DIG

1 A CHINESE MAPLE (*ACER BUERGERIANUM*) HAD FALLEN OVER, CREATING A NATURAL RAFT.

2 THE RATHER BIZARRE RAFT CAN BE CLEARLY SEEN HERE.

3 PART OF THE RAFT'S BASE SHOWING GOOD CURVES. THIS PIECE WAS REMOVED AND PLANTED.

4 THE NEWLY POTTED TREE SETTLES INTO ITS TEMPORARY HOME AND IS LEFT TO RECOVER.

5 FOUR YEARS LATER, THE NEW APEX AND BRANCHES ARE SHOWING GOOD GROWTH.

6 SIX YEARS ON, THE BUDDING BONSAI HAS DEVELOPED EVEN FURTHER.

STARTING WORK

Finding the bonsai within

Bonsai is both a practical and a visual art form in which the process is as important as the final result. This chapter demonstrates the art at the heart of bonsai practice: to seek, to find and to reveal the hidden qualities intrinsic to a plant or tree.

▶ REDUCING THE ROOT MASS ◀

While your tree settles into its new environment, which takes a year or two, consider design options and do not just rush into training. Once it has recovered, pay close attention to the roots. The root ball must be reduced to fit into a pot, which is best done in several stages.

When you lift the tree from the box to repot it, the soil will fall away easily, leaving a mass of fine new roots hanging from the old ones protruding from the old soil. (Save some used soil to mix with the new, in order to retain the beneficial micro-organisms.) Hose away the rest of the old soil.

Now, examine where the new roots have grown from. Cut back some old thick roots without sacrificing too many new ones. Don't go overboard at this stage, you can always remove more roots the next time you repot. The purpose of this gradual process is to end up with thick nebari that stop just below the surface of the soil, where they become a mass of finer roots.

Root reduction during repotting

At the first repotting after collection, some of the thick roots can be cut back, leaving sufficient new feeding roots to support the plant. Such reduction takes place each time the tree is repotted, until the only thick roots remaining are the nebari. Once all thick roots have been removed, the root structure should look something like the illustration below. (Note how the nebari stop just below the level of the soil, where they are gradually replaced by younger, active roots.)

OPPOSITE *After two to three years, carefully executed pruning wounds gradually become completely covered over with fresh woody tissue.*

▶ SHORTENING BROADLEAVED TREES ◀

With almost all broadleaved trees, it is possible to cut off all the branches and grow new ones from the many new shoots that are produced. Some branches may be strategically placed and merely need to be shortened to encourage them to fork closer to the trunk.

Either way, you'll inevitably need to shorten the trunk. This must be done so that the cut is hidden from view and the transition from thick old trunk to thin new leader looks natural.

Select a point on the trunk that is between 15 and 20 per cent below the anticipated final height of the tree. At this point, there should be a branch emerging slightly, but not directly, towards the front. Some way below this find another branch pointing slightly to the rear.

The trick is to make a sloping cut between the upper branch and the lower one so that, when viewed from the front, the cut is hidden and the trunk appears to taper evenly between the two branches. The adjacent diagrams below illustrate this process.

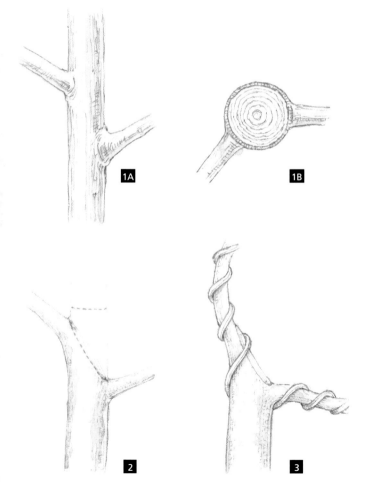

SHORTENING BROADLEAVED TREES

1 WHEN REDUCING THE HEIGHT OF A TALL TREE, SELECT TWO BRANCHES POSITIONED AS SHOWN: FROM THE FRONT (A) AND FROM ABOVE (B).

2 MAKE THE FIRST CUT STRAIGHT ACROSS THE TRUNK, JUST ABOVE THE UPPER BRANCH. THEN CARVE THE TRUNK (WITH A POWER TOOL) TO MAKE A SMOOTH TRANSITION FROM THE LOWER TO THE UPPER BRANCH. MAKE THIS CHAMFERED SECTION SLIGHTLY CONCAVE.

3 NOW WIRE THE UPPER BRANCH AND BEND IT UPWARD SO THAT ITS ANGLE FOLLOWS THE LINE OF THE CHAMFERED CUT. WHEN VIEWED FROM THE FRONT, THE CUT IS NOT SEEN AT ALL. ALSO, THE TRANSITION BETWEEN THE THICK ORIGINAL TRUNK AND THE NEW LEADER WILL LOOK QUITE SMOOTH AND PERFECTLY NATURAL.

▶ SHORTENING CONIFERS ◀

With conifers, you can't just remove all the branches and grow new ones. Without foliage to draw sap from the roots, the tree will die. However, you may wish to shorten the trunk. You can try same technique as for broadleaved trees, but not all conifers heal well, and the bark may die back around the cut.

A more visually exciting way to shorten the trunk of a conifer would be to make a *jin*. This simulates a tree that, in the past, has been struck by lightning.

Jins are a common sight on tall trees in wild, exposed areas and they are an image frequently used in bonsai.

TOP LEFT *The top of this hornbeam (Carpinus spp.) bonsai was created by shortening a 3m (10ft) tree and training in a new leader 12 years ago. Now, from the front it is difficult to see where this was done.*

TOP RIGHT *From the back, however, one can see that the cut has not yet healed entirely.*

SHORTENING A CONIFEROUS TREE

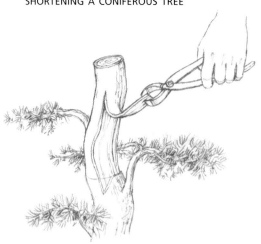

1 CUT THROUGH THE UNWANTED SECTION OF TRUNK, ABOVE THE ANTICIPATED FINAL HEIGHT OF THE TREE. CUT A RING ROUND THE TRUNK, ABOVE A BRANCH, BUT BELOW THE FINAL HEIGHT OF THE TREE. PEEL OFF THE BARK ON THE UNWANTED SECTION OF TRUNK.

3 KEEP PEELING AWAY SLIVERS OF WOOD UNTIL YOU ARE LEFT WITH A NATURAL-LOOKING IRREGULARLY POINTED *JIN*. NOW YOU CAN WIRE TRAIN THE TOP BRANCH TO FORM A ROUNDED APEX.

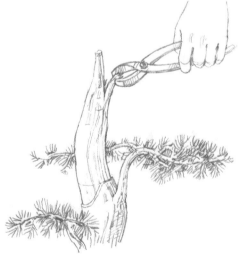

2 CRUSH THE EDGE OF THE CUT WITH PLIERS AND PEEL AWAY THE WOOD IN THIN SLIVERS. WORK CAREFULLY, OR YOU WILL DAMAGE THE BARK BELOW THE *JIN*.

ABOVE *Trees with* **jins** *and* **sharis** *are a common reaction to the harshness of a mountain environment. Without the ability to shed branches, most of these trees would not survive.*

▶ THE SIGNIFICANCE OF DEADWOOD ◀

Dead branches and sections of trunks stripped of their bark and bleached by the sun, are a common sight on conifers the world over. Whether on the Bristlecone Pines of California, the junipers of Japan or the towering spruce trees of the far north, these are skeletal reminders of the trees' struggle against a harsh environment. They add an air of antiquity and strength, like the wrinkled brow of an old peasant who sniffs the wind and knows whether it will snow, or rain.

The inclusion of *jins* and *sharis* endow a bonsai with similar properties, making a young tree appear ancient. In some cases, the deadwood is the focal point of the bonsai. Massive naked trunks with swirling movement, speckled with remains of long-lost branches, etched and bleached by wind, rain and sun.

Winding up this tortured trunk, there is a living vein: the sole link between the roots and the lush green canopy. The visual contrast between the red-brown bark, green foliage, and the silvery jins and sharis, is stunning. This contrast is echoed by the spiritual contrast between the green vigour of the foliage which hugs the bone-like deadwood.

ABOVE *The sprawling trunks of ancient junipers in a Japanese garden. These are the images that are reflected in many Driftwood Style bonsai.*

Such masterpieces are usually created from wild mountain plants but it's perfectly possible to make something similar from any substantial conifer. You may have a tree that has, for example, lost its branches on one side, or one whose trunk was carelessly shortened, leaving an ugly wound.

When you embark on the creation of a *Sharimiki* or 'Driftwood' Style bonsai, don't first consider the final branch layout, or even the overall design. These should be moulded to harmonize with the focus of the image: the deadwood. So concentrate on its size, shape and texture.

TOP *The intricate pattern of the grain is gradually exposed as the elements erode the deadwood.*

▸ CREATING DEADWOOD ◂

First, consider the future branch arrangement and the overall design. You must leave ample direct vascular links between the roots and the branches, or the tree will die. The vascular connection will usually be in a more or less straight line. Sometimes a trunk will become twisted, so that the vein will follow a spiral course. By studying the trunk you should be able to trace the vital connections. If you're lucky enough to have a tree that already has natural deadwood, it will help you locate the vascular connections, and will also aid you in visualizing the finished design.

Once you know which areas of bark must remain intact, decide how much of the rest you can safely remove. This decision is aesthetic. Bear in mind that the roots below the deadwood are no longer needed by the tree and can be included in the deadwood area.

Don't be too ambitious at first. Once bark is stripped, it cannot be replaced. With chalk, mark the edges of the area you think you would like to strip, then put another line some way inside the first. Strip the inner area first. If you want to increase the deadwood, do so in stages, coming back to it every month or so. This will give the tree time to adjust.

Shaping deadwood

If you wire and shape a newly-made *jin* and leave the wire in place for a couple of years, you'll be delighted to find that the *jin* will stay put when the wire is removed. However, you'll be dismayed to discover that it has returned to its original position after the first rain!

If you want to centre the design of a bonsai around a *jin* of a particular shape, you must wire the branch while it's still growing and wait until it is firm, before making the *jin*. This requires some forward planning.

A too-smooth, featureless surface might look as though the bark had been very recently

1 The imaginary conifer (above) has an interesting trunk, but only one branch and an ugly pruning wound, which makes it a prime candidate for the deadwood style. Two lines have been marked on the bark with chalk, the outer being the proposed margin of the deadwood area and the inner, the area that is to be stripped first.

2 The entire area has been stripped, and texture has been added to the otherwise smooth surface. (It is important to remember that the direct vascular connections of the tree must not be severed or the tree will die. A study of the trunk will give you clues and make it easier to trace the vital links.)

ABOVE *Natural* sharis *have a character that is inimitable. A degree of patience and creative carving, however, will allow you to approximate the original.*

stripped. It would look much more convincing it the wood had a fissured, rough, weather-beaten texture. Texture can be created by peeling away the wood, sliver by sliver. Patterns will develop as the grain weaves between old knots and hollows. Make some of the areas deeper than others, and leave some fairly smooth.

To reshape deadwood drastically, invest in an electric carving tool. Practise on bits of old wood before you launch an assault on a delicate bonsai. Vary the texture convincingly by using a variety of different bits. Try to ensure that the whorls and shapes you carve follow the natural grain, because the wood will crack along the grain when it dries. If the cracks and carved shapes appear to be in conflict, the look of the tree will be spoiled.

Preserving deadwood

Having put all that effort into your work of art, don't let it rot and don't let it go dark grey or spotted with algae. Apply a lime sulphur compound to the wood. This is an old recipe for spraying fruit trees in winter, and is a good fungicide. As the foul-smelling liquid soaks into the wood, it leaves a deposit of calcium on the surface. This dries to silvery white, imitating the bleaching effect of the sun.

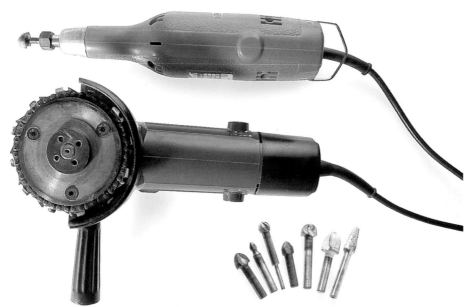

ABOVE *Heavy-duty power tools can save hours of hand carving. Remember to use hand and eye protection.*
TOP *Painting* jins *and* sharis *with lime sulphur is a rather smelly business but its preserving and bleaching effect is essential.*

▸ NOTES ON DESIGN ◂

When you deal with mature plants, you have to work with what nature has provided. Conforming to classical bonsai design criteria is usually impossible, because the trunk and much of the branch configuration is fixed, and totally beyond one's power to alter.

Rather than attempt to mould the tree into a predetermined style, you have to seek out the 'bonsai within'. Take your time. Your tree will enjoy being left in peace for a while, to recover from pruning or transplanting, so use this time to think about the bonsai it might become!

First, study the trunk line from every aspect and at all practical inclinations. Consider its dynamic, its movement. Does the trunk have a directional thrust? Does it suggest a history of strong winds or one of the oppressive weight of snow? Is the trunk angular or coiled in some way? Can it be tilted to become a Slanting bonsai, or even a Cascade?

While you are weighing up these possibilities, keep the nebari in mind. Any new changes in the trunk's inclination can cause good surface roots to be buried, while bad ones might to be pushed up above the soil level.

Discovering the best possibilities offered by the trunk takes priority over selecting the best view of the nebari. If these are ugly, see if there are more roots directly below the offending ones. Perhaps they are substantial enough to continue feeding that side of the tree if the unsightly roots were removed, made into *jins*, or hollowed out.

A tree is dictated by the character and inclination of the trunk, which records all of its history, age, stage, location and vigour. It, and it alone, will indicate what the eventual shape and size should be, and how the branches should be organized. A straight, upright trunk calls for neat, smoothly ramifying branches, that are very evenly distributed.

ABOVE *Thick, dead branches or less than ideally-shaped trunks can be much improved by subtle carving and shaping with power tools. Hand-held carving gouges are difficult to handle and place great strain on the tree.*

The same trunk, inclined at 30 degrees, indicates the fierce action of strong wind, so that the implied instability of the trunk has to be countered, both visually and horticulturally, by a more asymmetrical branch structure.

By a happy coincidence, most species that have stiff, inflexible branches are broadleaved trees. Conifers, which would die if their limbs were all removed, have very flexible branches that can easily be trained to conform to even the most oddly bizarre of trunk shapes.

When considering the eventual, overall shape, always seek out the smallest, neatest and most compact option (unless what you are aiming for is in the Literati style, of course). This will make the trunk appear proportionally thicker, which makes for an older-looking tree. Be sure to retain just the minimum number of branches which will be able to support the necessary foliage to complete the design. And be certain to allow sufficient space between the branches to prevent the tree from becoming a solid mass of unrelieved green when it is in full leaf.

Take your time; with bonsai there is no rush. The joy lies not in the finished product but in the pleasurable process. With this art, the deepest satisfaction is derived from dreaming, from watching your bonsai as it is refined and developed, year after year.

It is important to:
○ Work slowly, resting every few minutes to contemplate what you have achieved.
○ Always wear proper eye protection when using power tools!

ABOVE *As the sun and rain go to work on the newly carved wood the texture will slowly mellow, and the effect will become more natural in appearance.*

▸ PUTTING YOUR SKILLS INTO PRACTICE ◂

All the advice in the world can only outline the most basic principles of bonsai design and creation to a limited extent. To get the true message across, there's nothing like seeing those principles and processes put into practice. Here are three practical examples of making three very different types of bonsai from the kind of plants that you should be able to purchase from any reliable garden nursery.

Cotoneaster horizontalis in the Cascade style

THE DENSITY AND FLEXIBILITY OF COTONEASTER MAKES IT IDEAL FOR SMALLER BONSAI.

1 THE SAMPLE PLANT WAS SELECTED FOR ITS MANY BRANCHES AND ITS VERY VIGOROUS GROWTH.

2 SOIL WAS SCRAPED AWAY TO REVEAL THE FULL EXTENT OF THE TRUNK AND TO FIND SOME THICKER ROOTS TO USE AS *NEBARI*.

3 NOW YOU CAN BEGIN TO DETERMINE THE BEST FRONT AND PLANTING ANGLES. THE ROOTS ARE WRAPPED IN PLASTIC TO KEEP THEM MOIST.

4 MOST OF THE BRANCHES HAVE BEEN CUT AWAY, LEAVING ONLY THOSE THAT ARE NEEDED FOR DEVELOPMENT.

5 A CASCADE BONSAI IS PROPPED UP ON ONE SIDE TO ENCOURAGE THE TYPICAL GROWTH PATTERN. OVER THE NEXT FEW YEARS, LATERAL BRANCHES WILL BE SHAPED. THE TREE WILL BE PLANTED IN A CASCADE POT IN SPRING.

5

Cedrus Brevifolia in the slanting style

THIS CYPRIAN CEDAR HAS BEEN SELECTED FOR ITS TINY BLUE-GREEN NEEDLES AND THE FACT THAT IT IS TOUGH.

1 THE TREE IS READY FOR TRAINING. THE TRUNK HAS BEEN EXPOSED AND THE ROOTS PROTECTED WITH PLASTIC.

2 HAVING DECIDED ON THE PREFERRED PLANTING ANGLE, STRONG WIRE HAS BEEN CAREFULLY APPLIED TO THE TRUNK AND SOME SHAPE HAS GRADUALLY BEEN INTRODUCED.

3 THE UPPER PART OF THE TRUNK WAS NOT NEEDED, SO IT HAS BECOME A *JIN*. THE NEW *JIN* IS SHAPED BY PEELING AWAY SOME OF THE WOOD AND THEN BLEACHING WITH A LIME SULPHUR SOLUTION.

4 THE MAKINGS OF A FINE BONSAI, HELPED BY THE SLANTED BLOCK OF WOOD FIXED AT AN ANGLE TO SUPPORT IT. NOW IT IS POSSIBLE TO IMAGINE HOW IT IS GOING TO LOOK IN A FEW YEARS TIME, WHEN ALL THE BRANCHES HAVE FILLED OUT A LITTLE AND IT HAS BEEN POTTED UP.

Juniperus Chinensis in the raft style

THE CHINESE JUNIPER IS PERHAPS THE MOST VERSATILE OF ALL SPECIES SUITABLE FOR BONSAI.

1 THE CHOSEN PLANT LOOKS, AT FIRST, LIKE AN UNINSPIRING BUSH.

2 THE PLANT IS LAID ON ONE SIDE WITH MOST OF THE BRANCHES ON THE UPPERMOST ELEVATION.

3 THE TWO MAIN TRUNKS ARE CURVED WITH HEAVY WIRE. PATCHES OF BARK ARE REMOVED ON WHAT WILL EVENTUALLY BE THE UNDERSIDE. IN TIME, NEW ROOTS WILL APPEAR FROM AROUND THESE WOUNDS.

4 NOW ALL THE BRANCHES ARE WIRED VERTICALLY WITH HEAVY WIRE, TO FORM THE TRUNKS OF THE FUTURE RAFT-STYLE BONSAI ARRANGEMENT. THE CURVES IN THE ORIGINAL, HORIZONTAL TRUNKS CREATE A SENSE OF PERSPECTIVE.

5 PLANTED IN ITS TEMPORARY TRAINING BOX, THE UNINSPIRING BUSH HAS BECOME A MAGNIFICENT FOREST. AS THE SMALL BRANCHES GAIN STRENGTH, THEY TOO, WILL BE SHAPED WITH WIRE.

5

DIRECTORY

Plants that are good bonsai subjects

Practically any plant can be used to create an attractive bonsai but there are some species which respond better than others and that will reward their owners amply for the care and attention they lavish on them. This guide will help you to choose the right type of tree to suit the environment and conditions you are able to provide for it.

▸ HARDY SPECIES ◂

Acer buergerianum – Trident Maple

TRIDENT MAPLE ROOTS CAN BE DESTROYED BY REPEATED FREEZE/THAW CYCLES IN WINTER. SOIL SHOULD BE KEPT MOIST, BUT NOT WET, IN COLD WEATHER.

Summer placement Partial shade; protect from the afternoon sun, particularly in the hottest part of the year. Keep the roots cool by shading the pot.
Winter placement Shelter from wind and rain. Aim to keep the temperature constant, at above -5°C (23°F).
Feeding and watering Water abundantly in summer, less in winter. In the growing phase, feed with a balanced fertilizer and, in late summer, use a low-nitrogen plant food to harden off young shoots.
Wiring In mid-summer, after defoliation, or in late winter/early spring. Take care, because branches and hardened shoots are brittle and snap easily. With Trident Maples it is always best to wire-train shoots while they are still green.

Pruning Branches in autumn or late winter. Shoots as necessary throughout the summer; cut back to one or two pairs of leaves.
Repotting Every year or two. Use either pure Japanese Akadama soil or a mix of rounded grit and organic matter.

ABOVE RIGHT *Acer buergerianum* (Trident Maple).
LEFT *A Fukien Tea Tree* (Carmona microphylla) *in the Root-in-Rock style.*

Acer palmatum – Japanese Maple

LEAVES ARE EASILY BURNED BY SUN AND DRY WINDS IN SUMMER, ESPECIALLY IF THE ROOTS ARE TOO DRY.

Summer placement Partial or full shade, specially in the afternoon, when the sun is hottest. Protect from wind all year round.

Winter placement Japanese Maples will survive long periods of freezing if they are not exposed to cold winds, which will kill the small twigs. Keep temperatures above -10°C (14°F). Maples can leaf out too early if they are allowed to become warm in winter, even in the dark. This can exhaust the tree.

Feeding and watering Water frequently in summer. Little and often is better than allowing the soil to dry between drenchings. Use a balanced fertilizer all growing season and low-nitrogen in late summer to harden off young shoots.

Wiring Late winter or early spring. Young shoots can be wired in summer while they are still very flexible. Older branches can become brittle, and snap easily at their bases.

Pruning Branches in autumn or late winter. Shoots, as necessary, throughout the summer. Cut back to one or two pairs of leaves. Thin out clusters of shoots regularly, to maintain smooth branch and twig lines for winter enjoyment.

Repotting Every two to three years. Pure Japanese Akadama soil is best for these trees, but they will grow in any well-drained soil.

ABOVE *Acer palmatum* (Japanese Maple).

Cotoneaster horizontalis – Cotoneaster

 COTONEASTER IS NORMALLY EVERGREEN AND HAS SMALL WHITE FLOWERS THAT OPEN FULLY.

Summer placement Likes full sun. Can be kept indoors near a window for a week or two at a time.

Winter placement Outside, until the temperature falls below -5°C (23°F), then in a shed or garage.

Feeding and watering Feed a half-strength balanced fertilizer in spring and low nitrogen from mid-summer until autumn. Water sparingly all year. Cotoneasters naturally grow in rocky mountainous areas and hate having wet roots.

Wiring At any time, as the branches are flexible.

Pruning Cotoneasters are extremely dense and need regular trimming throughout the summer. In early spring, further thinning can be carried out, and branches can be pruned. Exposing new wounds to frost can cause drastic die-back of the surrounding bark.

Repotting Every two to four years. Use 70 per cent grit and 30 per cent organic matter or Akadama.

ABOVE *Cotoneaster horizontalis* (Cotoneaster).

Cryptomeria japonica – Temple Cedar

 CRYPTOMERIA DO NOT LIKE HAVING THEIR ROOTS IN DRY SOIL. OVERCROWDED SHOOTS WILL LEAD TO DIE-BACK OF LARGE AREAS.

Summer placement Full sun or even partial shade. (Shade, if you cannot water twice a day in hot weather.)

Winter placement Outside, until the temperature falls below -5°C (23°F), then move to a shed or garage.

Feeding and watering Water evenly in order to keep the soil constantly just damp.

Wiring Summer or autumn, after pruning. Wire may have to be re-applied several times before thicker branches set.

Pruning Branches in autumn. Trim shoots to keep the tree as neat as is required, and then thin out the congested areas towards the middle of summer.

Repotting This is necessary every two to four years. Use a slightly acid soil, which comprises at least 70 per cent coarse organic matter, the remainder can be grit.

ABOVE *Cryptomeria japonica* (Temple Cedar).

Ginkgo biloba – Maidenhair Tree

A BRANCH MAY DIE BACK AFTER IT HAS BEEN PRUNED DURING A HOT OR A COLD SPELL. LEAVE THE STUMPS OF PRUNED BRANCHES INTACT UNTIL THE TREE HAS RECOVERED. THEY CAN THEN BE CUT.

Summer placement Sun or partial shade. If it is not practical to water the tree twice a day, shade both the tree and the container in the warm afternoons.

Winter placement In cold areas, outside unless the temperature drops below -5°C (23°F). To be safe, keep the ginkgos in a frost-free outhouse during winter.

Feeding and watering Water generously during the summer and keep the soil evenly moist in winter. Do not overfeed. Organic fertilizers are best for ginkgo.

Wiring Young ginkgo branches are flexible, rubbery even but when they are older, they become brittle. Wire in the summer, after the first growth has been established. Check the wires regularly, and timeously remove all those that appear to be getting a little too tight.

Pruning Branches in autumn or late winter. The shoots, as and when it is necessary, to keep the tree neat throughout the summer. Be sure to leave at least a small piece of stump, in order to prevent die-back.

Repotting Ginkgos will benefit from being repotted annually, using a very open soil. Akadama mixed with 30 per cent grit is ideal; or you could try substituting some coarse organic matter for some or all of the Akadama.

ABOVE *Gingko biloba* (Maidenhair Tree).

Juniperus chinensis var. sargentii – Chinese Juniper (Shimpaku)

ALTHOUGH TOLERANT OF DRY ROOTS OCCASIONALLY, IT WILL DIE IF KEPT TOO DRY FOR TOO LONG. THESE TREES STAY GREEN, AND APPEAR TO BE ALIVE, FOR UP TO SIX MONTHS AFTER THEIR DEATH!

Summer placement Full sun or partial shade. Partial shade will improve their colour, but will also serve to encourage somewhat looser growth.

Winter placement Outside, or in an unheated greenhouse in cold weather. Shimpaku will grow slowly all winter if they are kept in good light and above 10°C (50°F).

Feeding and watering Apply a balanced fertilizer from spring until late summer. Continue to feed at one-quarter strength throughout winter, if the tree is still growing.

Wiring At any time, provided the weather remains mild. Remove wire and re-apply as necessary, every six months.

Pruning Prune branches in autumn or late winter. Pinch out growing tips constantly throughout the growing season. Cut the fatter, extending shoots back to healthy side shoots, to keep the tree's vigour in check.

Repotting Every two to four years. Use 50/50 grit and Akadama, or coarse organic matter. Add some natural charcoal and a little chopped sphagnum moss to the soil to improve root health and foliage colour.

ABOVE *Juniperus chinensis var. sargentii* (Chinese Juniper, or Shimpaku).

Juniperus rigida –
Needle Juniper

WATERLOGGING WILL KILL NEEDLE JUNIPERS. THE YOUNG SHOOTS ARE VERY SOFT BUT THE NEEDLES ARE VICIOUS, SO BE PREPARED FOR SOME PAIN WHEN WIRING!

Summer placement In full sun.

Winter placement Outside, but sheltered from the bitterest winds. Move to an unheated greenhouse, shed or garage when the temperature falls below -10°C (14°F).

Feeding and watering
Water moderately all year round, keeping the soil moist but not saturated. Feed moderately with a balanced fertilizer all growing season. (Overfeeding will result in weak, sappy growth.)

Wiring As with Shimpaku, at any time, provided the weather remains mild. Remove the wire and re-apply when necessary, every six months.

Pruning Prune branches in autumn. Cut the growing shoots back to two or three buds as they grow in summer. The buds form at the base of each needle.

Repotting Every three or four years. Don't prune away too many fine roots. Use a gritty soil with some coarse organic matter. Adding a little charcoal and some chopped fresh sphagnum moss to the soil will help to maintain healthy roots.

ABOVE *Juniperus rigida* (Needle Juniper).

Malus spp. – Crab Apple

CRAB APPLES OCCUR NATURALLY IN DEEP, FERTILE VALLEY SOIL, SO THEY PREFER A DEEP POT AND COOL ROOTS. THEY NEED A PERIOD OF FREEZING WEATHER TO STAY HEALTHY AND PERFORM AT THEIR BEST.

Summer placement Full sun or partial shade. Shade pots in hot weather to keep the roots cool.

Winter placement Outside but protected from cold winds. Move to a garage or shed if temperatures remain below -15°C (5°F), for more than a week. Bring trees back outside as soon as the temperature rises to just below freezing. Do not let the tree become too warm, as this might induce premature flowering. Although the flowers are not usually harmed by frost, the tree may become exhausted if it does not get all the dormancy it requires.

Feeding and watering Water copiously in the spring and summer, less in winter.

Wiring Wire in summer to build a basic branch arrangement. Crab apple branches are thick and fleshy, and the bark is easily rubbed off with careless wiring. It's better to develop heavy branches by pruning, rather than by wiring.

Pruning Prune branches in autumn if necessary. Cut back last year's shoots to a convenient bud after flowering. Allow subsequent growth to flourish freely until late summer, then cut back, leaving between two and four buds, Remember that the buds at the base of each shoot are the following year's flower buds.

Repotting Every two or three years. Use a heavier soil than for most trees, with some organic matter and/or Akadama. Also, use a pot that seems a bit too large.

ABOVE *Malus spp.* (Crab Apple), in winter.

Pinus parviflora – Japanese White Pine

WHITE PINES MUST HAVE A PERIOD OF FREEZING EACH WINTER IN ORDER TO REMAIN IN GOOD HEALTH.

Summer placement Full sun all day, although they will tolerate moderate shade.

Winter placement Outside, sheltered from cold winds. Grafted trees should be protected from the cold, especially from temperatures below -10°C (14°F).

Feeding and watering Water moderately in the summer, sparingly in winter, and then only if necessary. Use low nitrogen fertilizer until the new needles have spread, then feed with high nitrogen plant food until autumn.

Wiring Late summer and autumn.

Pruning Branches in autumn. New shoots must be shortened (or cut off completely in the congested areas) in mid-summer. Let the new, inner shoots gain strength for one or two years before cutting them away

Repotting Every three to five years. Use a very coarse gritty soil containing only about 20–30 per cent organic matter, or Akadama.

ABOVE *Pinus parviflora* (Japanese White Pine).

Pinus thunbergii – Japanese Black Pine

 THE JAPANESE BLACK PINE WILL NOT SURVIVE FOR VERY LONG IN SOIL THAT IS WATERLOGGED.

Summer placement In full sun, all day.

Winter placement Outside, but sheltered from the biting winds of winter. Black pines deteriorate if they don't get sufficient fresh air and cold during winter. If you must house yours in a building, then make sure the room is adequately ventilated and that the trees are well spaced out. Take the tree outside for a holiday whenever possible.

Feeding and watering Water sparingly at all times, even less when needles are maturing. Never allow soil to become waterlogged.

Feed with a low nitrogen fertilizer while the shoots (called 'candles') are extending, then switch to high nitrogen feed in late summer and autumn, to encourage the production of plenty of new buds.

Wiring In summer, after removing old needles and pinching new candles. Shoots are flexible, but often short and thick, which makes fine adjustments difficult.

Pruning Branches in autumn or late winter. Pinch, or cut off about two-thirds to three-quarters of each of the extending candles, as the needles begin to peel away.

Repotting Every three to five years. Use a very coarse and gritty soil (some people even use sand). Mixing a little pine needle mould into the soil will keep the tree in the peak of health.

ABOVE *Pinus thunbergii* (Japanese Black Pine).

Rhododendron indicum – Satsuki Azalea

TAKE CARE WHEN WIRING, BECAUSE THE BRANCHES ARE VERY BRITTLE. AZALEAS DO NOT GROW WELL IN SOIL THAT CONTAINS LIME. PLANTS WITH THIS CHARACTERISTIC ARE CALLED CALCIFUGES.

Pruning Prune branches and shoots in early summer, after flowering. Thin out dense areas, to allow the young inner shoots room to grow.

Repotting Every three years or so. If you water with hard tapwater (containing lime), repot more frequently. Use an ericaceous (lime-free), compost or Japanese Kanuma soil.

Summer placement
Partial or full shade, but the larger bonsai are able to tolerate some sun.

Winter placement
Azaleas are hardy but they don't like cold winds or having their roots frozen for prolonged periods. A cool, shaded greenhouse is the ideal spot in which to overwinter them.

Feeding and watering
Satsukis won't tolerate dry roots but they are not particularly thirsty. Water them only when necessary, keeping the soil evenly moist, all year round. Feed with a low nitrogen fertilizer in the growing season and top up with a light organic feed in winter.

Wiring Wire only when you cannot prune for shape. Only wire young shoots in summer, until you become more experienced, because the branches and older shoots break very easily.

ABOVE *Rhododendron indicum* (Satsuki Azalea).

Stuartia (Stewartia) monodelpha – Stuartia

STUARTIAS ARE CALCIFUGES – THEY WILL NOT TOLERATE LIME IN EITHER THEIR SOIL OR THEIR WATER.

Summer placement Partial shade for most of the summer. Move them into full sun towards the autumn, this helps to intensify their autumn colours.

Winter placement Keep outside until temperatures fall below -5°C (23°F), then move to a shed or garage.

Feeding and watering Water diligently, keeping the soil moist at all times but avoid waterlogging. Use only rainwater or lime-free tapwater. Use an ericaceous fertilizer (one that is made for acid-loving plants), during the growing season.

Wiring Autumn or late winter. Take care, as the bark is soft and is easily damaged.

Pruning Prune branches in autumn or early spring. Prune shoots back to one or two leaves, as necessary. Keep the branch framework open, to allow light and air to penetrate to the inner shoots. Although the flowers are too large to be of any value on a bonsai, some people like them. To induce flowering, treat as crab apples.

Repotting Every two to three years. Use an ericaceous organic compost, sifted to remove fine particles, mixed with 30 per cent grit. Make sure the grit doesn't contain any lime. Chicken grit, for example, often has a high lime content, as do some builders' sands. Always buy grit from the most reputable suppliers, or collect your own from sources that you know to be absolutely lime-free.

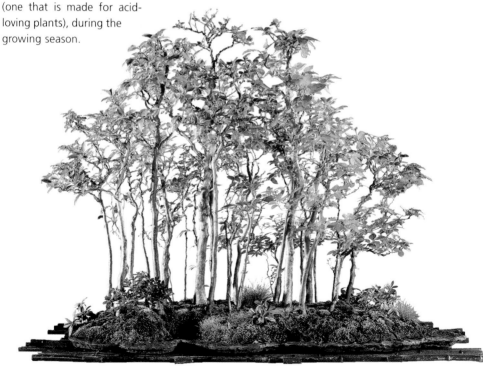

ABOVE *Stuartia monodelpha* or *Stewartia monodelpha*, commonly known as Stuartia.

Ulmus parvifolia – Chinese Elm

CHINESE ELMS KEPT INDOORS WILL LOSE THEIR LEAVES IN RESPONSE TO CHANGES IN LOCATION, SO FIND A SPOT YOUR TREE LIKES, AND LEAVE IT THERE. NEVER USE SYSTEMIC TREATMENTS ON CHINESE ELMS. THEY WILL LOSE THEIR LEAVES AND SOME YOUNG SHOOTS MAY DIE.

Summer placement Outside in full sun, inside near a window that provides good light but no direct sun.

Winter placement Indoors in a well-ventilated, cool room with good indirect light. Outdoors in an insulated shed. Keep at a temperature above -5°C (23°F).

Feeding and watering Water regularly but don't allow the soil to become saturated for long periods. Use a balanced fertilizer all growing season with the addition of a low-nitrogen feed in late summer.

Wiring Wire at any time. Branches thicken quickly in late summer, so keep an eye open for tight wires. Branches are supple but can separate at the base if pushed too far.

Pruning Branches in autumn or late winter. Shoots as necessary throughout the summer, be sure only to cut back to one or two leaves.

Repotting Best done every year or two. Always use Japanese Akadama soil (if possible) or a mixture of 70 per cent coarse organic matter and 30 per cent grit.

ABOVE *Ulmus parvifolia* (Chinese Elm).

Wisteria spp. – Wisteria

Some people have trouble getting wisterias to flower. Standing the pot in a dish of water, so that water seeps up through the drainage holes during summer, often does the trick! Flower buds will drop if the roots are too dry.

Summer placement Full sun, but shade the pots in very hot weather.

Winter placement Outside, or in a greenhouse in cold spells. Don't stand the pot in water in the wintertime.

Feeding and watering Water copiously in spring and summer, and keep soil very moist – but not saturated – in the winter months.

Wiring Autumn, after pruning. Little wiring should be needed, since whatever shaping is necessary can be achieved by pruning. Although the branches seem flexible at first, they do have an annoying habit of snapping without warning.

Pruning Cut back to a basic simple framework of branches immediately after flowering, and allow free growth of all the shoots for as long as possible. After that, cut all long shoots back to two or three buds, and thin out the crowded areas. Repeat as often as necessary during the growing season. Flower buds will begin to form on the stubs of the most recently pruned shoots.

Repotting Every two to four years. Use a slightly acid soil which is rich in organic matter.

ABOVE *Wisteria* (Wisteria).

Zelkova serrata –
Japanese Grey-Bark Elm /
Zelkova

Repotting Every two to three years. It is best to use Japanese Akadama soil or a mixture of 70 per cent coarse organic matter and 30 per cent grit.

BEWARE OF BONSAI MARKED 'ZELKOVA SINICA' – THESE ARE ALMOST ALWAYS CHINESE ELMS DELIBERATELY LABELLED TO MISLEAD, IN AN ATTEMPT TO AVOID IMPORT RESTRICTIONS.

Summer placement Either full sun or partial shade.

Winter placement Keep outside, sheltered from cold winds. Protect the zelkovas in a shed or a garage if the temperature threatens to remain below -10°C (14°F) for more than a few days at a time.

Feeding and watering Water daily in summer and keep soil moist in winter, but do not overwater at any time. Feed generously while the twigs are developing and sparingly when the tree is fully formed.

Wiring At any time. Branches are supple and will set in position quite quickly in the spring and summer.

Pruning Prune branches in autumn or late winter; shoots as necessary through the summer, then cut them back to one or two leaves.

ABOVE *Zelkova serrata* (Japanese Grey-Bark Elm *or* Zelkova).

Carmona microphylla (Ehretia buxifolia) – Fukien Tea

CARMONAS WILL DIE IF EXPOSED TO EVEN A SLIGHT FROST. IN SOME CASES, JUST A COLD DRAUGHT OF AIR COULD PROVE FATAL.

Summer placement Indoors near a bright window but not in direct sun. Or outdoors in partial shade.

Winter placement Keep above 15°C (60°F) for best results. Never below 5°C (41°F).

Feeding and watering Water copiously while growing, but ease off when growth slows down in winter. Feed sparingly with a balanced house-plant fertilizer.

Wiring At any time of the year. Branches can get brittle if the soil is wet.

Pruning At any time, but best towards the end of winter. Cut shoots as required to keep the tree looking neat.

Repotting Every two to three years. Use a soil with a very high organic content.

ABOVE *Carmona microphylla* or *Ehretia buxifolia* (Fukien Tea).

Celtis sinensis - Chinese Hackberry

 CELTIS ARE DECIDUOUS, AND MUST HAVE A PERIOD AT LEAST SIX WEEKS BELOW 5°C (41°F) – AND PREFERABLY BELOW FREEZING – TO INITIATE DORMANCY. WITHOUT PROPER DORMANCY, THE TREE WILL BECOME EXHAUSTED AND MIGHT DIE.

Summer placement
Likes sun. Keep outside, or near a window. Shade pots in hot weather.

Winter placement
Leave outside or place in a conservatory, provided the temperature remains at between -5°C and 5°C (23°F and 41°F).

Feeding and watering
Water generously during summer, but keep just moist while dormant. Feed regularly from spring to late summer. Use balanced fertilizer (for twig growth), and low nitrogen for both flowers and fruit.

Wiring When the plant is dormant.

Pruning In autumn or late winter before growth starts. Trim the shoots regularly in summer.

Repotting Every year or two, using only Japanese Akadama soil or a 50/50 mixture of grit and coarse organic matter.

ABOVE *Celtis sinensis* (Chinese Hackberry).

Ficus spp. – Figs

 MILKY WHITE LATEX POURS FROM PRUNING WOUNDS, SO IT'S BEST TO PRUNE FIGS IN WINTER WHEN THE SAP RISES MORE SLOWLY.

Summer placement Keep outside, in semi-shade or indoors near a light window but not in full sun.

Winter placement Keep above 15°C (60°F), though temperatures as low as 5°C (41°F) should be safe.

Feeding and watering Water well in summer and keep soil moist in winter. Feed regularly with a well balanced fertilizer in summer. Continue feeding at half strength if growth continues in winter.

Wiring At any time. Branches can thicken very rapidly, so watch out for wire cutting into the soft bark.

Pruning Possible at any time but best in winter to avoid excessive 'bleeding'. Wounds can be sealed by pressing lightly with a very hot knife blade.

Repotting Every two years at any time, but best in early spring, before growth starts. Keep warm after repotting, to encourage new roots. Use a free-draining soil with about 60 per cent organic matter.

ABOVE *Ficus* varieties (Figs).

Ligustrum sinensis – Privet

 SOIL THAT IS ALWAYS WET WILL EVENTUALLY CAUSE ROOT ROT.

Summer placement Indoors or out (in full sun or partial shade). If grown indoors in shade, keep the feeding and watering routines to a minimum.

Winter placement Indoors or out – move plant to a conservatory or cold room if the weather freezes for more than a few days.

Feeding and watering Water often, but only if the soil feels dry. Feed with balanced fertilizer in summer, and at one-quarter strength in winter, if buds are still opening.

Wiring At any time. Branches can swell quickly, so check regularly for wire that is becoming too tight. Branches are brittle but shoots remain flexible for three or four years. If you snap a thin branch while wiring, it should survive and mend itself within a year or so, provided at least half the branch is still intact. Privet shoots grow at all angles, so branch shaping can be done by pruning.

Pruning At any time. Trim new shoots to one pair of leaves throughout the growing period. Privet is normally so dense and vigorous that you will probably find it necessary to thin out overcrowded areas, and cut away adventitious shoots, several times a year.

Repotting This should be done every two years at least. It is best to use a gritty soil which includes at least 50 per cent coarse organic matter. The usually fine feeding roots are somewhat coarse and stringy (they resemble miniature spaghetti). They have a tendency to regenerate with great rapidity, so make sure that you prune the roots quite thoroughly each time you repot.

ABOVE *Ligustrum senensis* (Privet).

Myrtus – Myrtle

 MYRTLE IS DECIDUOUS, SO IT IS ESSENTIAL THAT IT HAS A PERIOD OF DORMANCY EACH YEAR, OR IT WILL DIE.

Summer placement Outdoors, either in full sun or partial shade. Indoors, in good light near a window but not directly in strong sun through a pane of glass.

Winter placement In a cool conservatory or a cold room where the temperature is constantly between 5°C and 10°C (41°F and 50°F), to induce dormancy.

Feeding and watering Water regularly but do not allow the soil to remain saturated. Try to use either rainwater or lime-free tap water. Feed, during the growing season, with a good balanced fertilizer (this is best fed at half strength).

Wiring When dormant.

Pruning Branches during dormancy. Trim the shoots to maintain shape during summer, and slice off any unwanted adventitious buds before they open.

Repotting Every two years. Use an ericaceous (acid) compost, sifted to remove fine particles and mixed 50/50 with grit.

ABOVE *Myrtus* (Myrtle).

Olea spp. – Olive

Olives don't produce new shoots around the cut when you prune a branch. If you want new shoots, leave the branch longer than you eventually want it to be, and shorten it later, after the new shoots have matured.

Summer placement As hot and as sunny as you like, indoors or out.

Winter placement Keep above 5°C (41°F), in good light.

Feeding and watering Water infrequently, but don't allow the soil to become bone-dry between waterings. Feed a balanced fertilizer, at half strength in spring and summer. Also in winter, if the tree is still growing.

Wiring Best not to. The branches are so brittle that there's little point in even trying to train them. Branch shape can be easily achieved by pruning alone.

Pruning In spring and summer.

Repotting Every three or four years. Cut heavy roots back as hard as you like, but retain about 50 per cent of the fine roots. Use a very gritty soil with about 30 per cent organic matter. In the warmer parts of Europe, landscape architects are able to dig out massive, ancient olives from the mountains and plant them in parks and gardens. These might be many hundreds of years old but they do survive drastic root pruning and transplantation as if it were nothing much.

ABOVE *Olea spp.* (Olive).

Pistacia terebinthus – Pistachio

 ALMOST ALL HEALTH PROBLEMS IN THIS SPECIES ARE ASSOCIATED WITH THE STATE OF THE ROOTS. KEEP THE SOIL CONSTANTLY MOIST.

Summer placement Full sun or semi-shade in hot weather. Protect from direct summer sun through glass.

Winter placement Keep above 10°C (50°F), and well away from draughts. Mist-spray daily.

Feeding and watering Water carefully, making sure the soil is thoroughly damp at all times, but not permanently saturated. Feed moderately with a good balanced fertilizer in the summer and stop feeding when the tree stops growing.

Wiring In the late summer or the early autumn, when the branches are less likely to be brittle.

Pruning At any time. However, please note that the bark crushes very easily, so be sure that the tools you use are are clean and particularly sharp.

Repotting Best done every two or three years. Use soil that comprises 60 per cent organic matter, mixed with grit.

ABOVE *Pistacia terebinthus* (Pistachio).

Podocarpus macrophyllus – Chinese Yew

PODOCARPUS DO NOT LIKE THEIR ROOTS TO BE DISTURBED AND OFTEN DETERIORATE FOR SOME TIME AFTER THEY ARE REPOTTED.

Summer placement Outdoors in full sun or indoors near a bright window, but take care to never expose them to direct sun shining through the glass.

Winter placement Keep in good light, at above 5°C (41°F). Exposure to freezing is risky, but is not invariably fatal.

Wiring Best avoided, because of the easily fractured branches and dense leaves.

Pruning At any time. Always use very sharp tools to avoid mashing the delicate fibrous shoots and branches.

Repotting Every three to four years. This must be done carefully. Don't remove more than 20 per cent of the existing roots.

Feeding and watering
Water generously while growing, but reduce water when growth stops in winter. Feed regularly with a good, balanced houseplant fertilizer.

ABOVE *Podocarpus macrophyllus* (Chinese Yew).

Punica granatum – Pomegranate

 THE FLOWERS ARE PRODUCED ON SHORT SPURS ON THE PREVIOUS YEAR'S SHOOTS, SO BE CAREFUL NOT TO PRUNE THESE AWAY!

Summer placement Full sun indoors or out. Shade the pot if the trees are exposed to sun shining through a glass pane.

Winter placement Maintain above 5°C (41°F). Keep in good light as long as any leaves remain.

Feeding and watering Water well and don't let the soil dry out completely.

Water demand is high when the flower buds or fruit are swelling.

Wiring Very carefully in winter. Branches are extremely brittle and snap very easily.

Pruning During winter. Ensure that you leave the flowering spurs on the old wood.

Repotting In early spring, before the new shoots emerge. Use either Japanese Akadama soil or a 50/50 mixture of grit and coarse organic matter.

ABOVE *Punica granatum* (Pomegranate).

Sageretia theezans – Sageretia

 SAGERETIAS WILL NOT TOLERATE COLD DRAUGHTS OR A CONSTANTLY DRY ATMOSPHERE. IN CENTRALLY HEATED HOMES, USE A DOMESTIC HUMIDIFIER, OR SPRAY TREES SEVERAL TIMES A DAY.

Summer placement Partial shade, indoors or out. Surrounding the tree with other, larger plants will help to create local humidity.

Winter placement Keep above 15°C (60°F) and away from draughts. They enjoy a humid atmosphere.

Feeding and watering
Water copiously when the tree is growing. Keep the soil moist in winter. Feed with a good fertilizer while the tree is growing, but stop when growth slows down in the autumn.

Wiring Too brittle for wires. So develop branch shape by judicious pruning.

Pruning This may be done at any time. The wood is rock hard, so when you prune, be certain that your tools are not only very clean, but sharp as well.

Repotting Every two to three years. Use 70 per cent organic matter and 30 per cent grit; put into a deep pot.

ABOVE *Sageretia theezans* (Sageretia).

Serissa foetida – Serissa

 THE NAME REFERS TO THE FETID SMELL GIVEN OFF BY THE BARK AND ROOTS OF THIS TREE. PLEASE NOTE THAT IF YOU SPRAY THE TREE WHILE IT IS IN BLOOM, THIS MAY CAUSE THE FLOWERS TO FADE PREMATURELY.

Summer placement Outdoors in partial shade, or indoors, close to a window. Avoid direct sun through glass.

Winter placement Keep in good light, at above 12°C (54°F), warmer if possible. If the plant is kept in a heated room, spray several times a day.

Feeding and watering Water copiously. Stand the pot in a tray of water to keep the soil soaked in summer, but don't do this in winter. Feed with a well-balanced fertilizer when they are growing fast. If growth stops in winter, they do not need to be fed at all.

Wiring At any time of year, but with care. The branches can be extrememly brittle, and the dense growth tends to make the wiring awkward. Branches can be easily developed by pruning alone.

Pruning At any time. Keep congested areas thinned to maintain vigour.

Repotting Every two to three years. Use a soil with a high organic content.

ABOVE *Serissa foetida* (Serissa).
OPPOSITE *In close up, moss and weathered bark create a landscape in miniature.*

Accent plant A separate planting of seasonal grasses or small herbaceous plants displayed with a formal bonsai.

Akadama Japanese clay-like soil with perfect characteristics for bonsai.

Anneal Softening wire by heating it to red-hot and allowing it to cool slowly.

Apically dominant A plant that concentrates a lot of energy in upward growth.

Bankan Twisted Trunk Style. Unnatural and, thankfully, now seldom used.

Bunjan Literati Style: tall, slender trunk with ample movement and minimal foliage. Reflects the brush strokes of Chinese calligraphy.

Calcined clay Clay that has been baked to stabilize the granules. It is able to absorb large volumes of water without breaking down and is used as a soil conditioner.

Calcifuges Plants that will not tolerate lime in their soil or in their water.

Cambium A thin layer of cell tissue between the bark and wood that produces new xylem and phloem, thus aiding growth.

CEC Cation Exchange Capacity – the ability of a material to absorb nutrients from soil water and release them to the roots as required.

Cleft grafts/crown grafts Quick method of grafting ornamental varieties onto stocks of stronger varieties. Commercially successful this often leaves ugly unions.

Chokkan Formal Upright Style, with a straight, trunk tapering from the base to the apex.

Cut paste A putty-like substance used to seal pruning wounds to promote healing.

Damping off A group of fungal diseases that attacks seedlings, causing them to collapse.

Dwarf A plant that is smaller than the average for its species, but otherwise similar.

Ericaceous Soil that contains no lime. Also plants of the heather family.

Fukinagashi Windswept Style, in which the tree looks as if it lives on a wind-blasted hill.

Growing on Allowing plants a period of free growth to strengthen them.

Han-kengai Semi-Cascade Style, in which the tree cascades below the rim of the pot.

Hardy Trees able to withstand winter frosts.

Hardwood cuttings Cuttings from shoots that have become woody, usually in autumn.

Heel A sliver of the parent branch that stays attached to a hardwood cutting.

Hokidachi Broom Style, in which the trunk is straight and the branches fan out to form a symmetrical, domed canopy.

Internode The section of a stem between the leaf nodes.

Ishitsuki Root-in-Rock Style, in which the rock acts as a container for the roots.

Jin A dead branch which has been removed, either naturally, or artificially. Can also be used as a verb. There is no English equivalent

Kabudachi Clump Style, in which the trunks are joined at the base. Usually made by cutting a single trunk to ground level, and training the many new shoots.

Kanuma Japanese volcanic clay which is excellent for growing azaleas.

Kengai Cascade Style, in which the tree cascades to below the base of the pot.

Layering Wrapping a deliberately wounded branch with a wad of sphagnum moss in order to induce the production of a new set of roots.

Leader The main, upward-growing shoot of a branch, or the continuation of the trunk.

Lignified A shoot or a root that has become woody as a plant matures.

Mame Mini-bonsai that will fit on the palm of your hand.

Moyogi Informal Upright Style featuring a curved, upright trunk.

Mycorrhizae Microscopic subterranean fungi which colonize plant roots and assist them in gathering nutrients and water in return for sugars manufactured by the host plant.

▶ GLOSSARY ◀

Neagari Exposed Root Style, in which the tree stands on a column of exposed roots.

Nebari Heavy roots which are visible above the surface of the soil.

Needle A long narrow stiff leaf with a hard texture, in which water loss is greatly reduced.

Netsunanari, Ikadabuki Raft Style, trunks of the bonsai are formed from branches of the true trunk, which is laid horizontally in the pot, and partially or entirely covered with soil.

NPK Abbreviation for a commonly used garden fertilizer containing varying proportions of nitrogen (N), phosphorus (P) and potassium (K).

Penjing Chinese art of miniature landscapes. A tree with a rock is *penjing*, not *punsai*.

Pricking out Planting newly germinated seedlings in individual containers.

Pot-bound Term used to describe a plant whose roots have filled all the available space in the pot, preventing further growth.

Propagator Commercial unit with container for soil and cuttings and a clear cover.

Pruning Cutting or pinching back branches, leaves or stems to control or remove unwanted growth and shape the plant.

Pumice Soft stone made from fine-pored lava.

Punsai Chinese pronunciation of the word we know as 'bonsai'.

Reverse osmosis The passage of water from within roots to the soil. It may be caused by an excessive concentration of fertilizer in the soil.

Rootburn The effect on roots of 'reverse osmosis' which may be caused by overfeeding with a rich fertilizer.

Rooting hormone Commercial preparations that some growers believe may be credited with an increase in the success rate of propagation from soft or hardwood cuttings.

Sekijôju Root-over-Rock Style, in which roots are clasped to a rock before they enter the soil.

Semi-ripe cuttings Cuttings from shoots that are just hardening, in mid- to late summer.

Shakan Slanting Style. A variation of the Upright Styles, with the trunk inclined to either the left or the right.

Shari An area of trunk from which bark has been removed, either naturally or artificially, by carving. (Similar to a jin.)

Sharimiki, Sabamiki Driftwood Style, in which deadwood is the major feature.

Shimpaku The Japanese term for the tree known in English as the Chinese Juniper.

Shohin Small bonsai, that are generally under 150mm (6in) tall.

Softwood cuttings Cuttings taken from young shoots that are still green. This is usually done in the early months of the summer.

Sôju Double-trunk Style, where a larger and smaller trunk are joined at the base.

Sphagnum moss Also known as bog moss, this highly absorbent moss is the best medium to use when air-layering.

Stratification The process of exposing the seeds of some hardy trees to extremely low temperatures, to stimulate germination

Suiseki Viewing stone. A stone resembling, for example, a mountain or a cliff. The stone is generally mounted on a plinth and used as an accent to complement a bonsai display.

Tokonoma An alcove in a traditional Japanese home. Used for displaying bonsai, it generally consists of the bonsai, an accent and a scroll. (Not to be confused with the Tokoname region of Japan, a notable supplier of bonsai pots.)

Trace elements Chemicals that plants only require in minute quantities. These are usually present in garden soil but are almost always absent from inert bonsai soils.

Woody A hardened plant stem that will not die off during dormancy or in winter.

Yamadori Wild trees that may be collected from open ground and trained as bonsai

Yose-ue Forest Style. Any number of trees planted together to resemble a forest.

▶ INDEX ◀

Numbers in *italics* represent
photographs or illustrations.

*A*cer palmatum (*see* Japanese Maple)
Acer palmatum 'chishio' (*see*
   Japanese Red Maple)
adventitious buds *16*, 17, 24, 28
air layering 24
Akadama (*see also* soil) 110, 112
American Larch 120
autumn leaves *25*, 29
azalea 96 (*see also* Satsuki Azalea)
*B*anyan Fig *20*
bark *22*, *23*
Bird's Nest Spruce *89*
branches 22–24, 34–35, 51, 119,
   128, 133, 136, 144, 152, 153
broadleaved trees 105, 133
shortening 144
buds 25, *26*, 27, 28–29
   apical 25, 28
   axillary 25, 27, 28
   (*see also*) adventitious buds
buying bonsai 44, 46–51
*C*alcifuge 55
cambium *22*, 23, 24
Caprinus betalus (*see* European
   Hornbeam)
Carmona microphylla (*see* Fukien
   Tea Tree)
Carpinus spp. (*see* Hornbeam)
Cedar, Cyprian 156–157
   Pencil 120
   Temple (*see* Temple Cedar)
Cedrus brevifolia (*see* Cedar,
   Cyprian)
Celtis sinensis (*see* Chinese
   Hackberry)
Chamaecyparis obtusa (*see* Hinoki
   Cypress)
Chinese bonsai culture 11
Chinese Elm 49, 63, 173

Chinese Hackberry 177
Chinese Juniper 45, 91, 92,
   158–159, 166
Chinese Yew 183
Common Privet 35
conifers 49, *138*, 105, 133, 153
   shortening 145, 146
Cotoneaster 154–155, 163
Cotoneaster horizontalis (*see*
   Cotoneaster)
Crab Apple 168
Cryptomeria japonica (*see* Temple
   Cedar)
cuttings 124–125
cypress, Swamp 120
*D*eadwood 147, 148, 149–151
   shaping 152–153
diseases 72, *73*
   (*see also* pests and diseases)
displaying bonsai 40–41
*E*hretia buxifolia (*see* Fukien Tea
   Tree)
elm *48*
*F*eeding 65–67, 68, 69
fertilizer 65, 66, 67, 68–69
Ficus Burtt-Davyi (*see* South African
   Veld Fig)
Ficus retusa (*see* Banyan Fig)
Ficus spp (*see* Figs)
Figs 49, 178
foliage (*see* leaves)
Fukien Tea Tree *160*, 161, 176
fungi 72, *73*, 74
*G*ingko biloba (*see* Maidenhair Tree)
grafts 133
growing new branches 85
*H*eartwood *22*, 22
Hinoki Cypress 14, 92
history of bonsai 12–13
Hornbeam (European) *12*, *145*
*I*ndoor bonsai 48
insects (*see* pests)

*J*apanese Black Pine 170
Japanese bonsai culture 11, 12–15
Japanese cut paste 51, 82, *83*
Japanese Grey-Bark Elm 175
Japanese Maple 112, 162
Japanese Red Maple *88*
Japanese White Pine *10*, 11, 169
jin 145, 146, 147, 149, 151
Juniper 112, *118*, 119, *139*, 147
   Californian 120
   Chinese (*see* Chinese Juniper)
   Sabina 120
   San Jose *118*, 119, 120
Juniperus chinensis var. sargentii
   (*see* Chinese Juniper)
Juniperus rigida (*see* Needle Juniper)
Juniperus scopulorum (*see* Rocky
   Mountain Juniper)
*K*anuma 110
*L*arch *42*, 43, 92, 120, 121
Larix laricini (*see* American Larch)
Larix spp. (*see* larch)
layering 126–127, 128
leaves 24–25, 29, 51, 119
light 60–62
Ligustrum lucidum (*see* Common
   Privet)
Ligustrum sinensis (*see* Privet)
lime 55
*M*aidenhair Tree 165
Malus spp. (*see* Crab Apple)
mame 32
Maple (*see also* Japanese Maple)
   Trident (*see* Trident Maple)
miniature bonsai (*see mame*)
mycorrhizae 74
Myrtle 180
Myrtus (*see* Myrtle)
*N*ebari 19, *32*, 50, 51, *132*, 133,
   136, 143
Needle Juniper 92, 167
nitrogen 66

▶ INDEX ◀

nutrients 65

Olea spp. (*see* Olive)

Olive 121, 181

organic fertilizer 67, 69, 111

osmosis 20–21

Pests and diseases 70–75

aphids *70*, 71

gall mites 71, *72*

insects 72

root aphids 71

spider mites 71

vine weevils 72

phloem *22*, 23, 24

phosphorus 66

photosynthesis 24–25

Picea abies var. nidiformis (*see* Bird's Nest Spruce)

pinching 25, 89–92

broadleaved trees 94

conifers 92–93

flowering bonsai 96

Juniper leaves 92

pine candles 91

techniques 90–91

timing 89

pines 49, 147

Pinus parviflora (*see* Japanese White Pine)

Pinus sylvestris (*see* Scots Pine)

Pinus thunbergii (*see* Japanese Black Pine)

Pistachio 182

Pistacia terebinthus (*see* Pistachio)

plant health 75

Podocarpus macrophyllus (*see* Chinese Yew)

Pomegranate 184

Port Jackson Fig 121

potassium 66

pots *104*, 105, *106–109*

Privet 179

propogation, young plants 122–125

proportion 32–35

pruning 25, 51, 82–88, 95, 105, 119

wounds 82–83, *142*, 143

Punica granatum (*see* Pomegranate)

Repotting 105–117, 137, 143

Rhodendron indicum (*see* Satsuki Azalea)

Rocky Mountain Juniper *30*, 31

roots 17, 18–21, 113, 114–115, 119, 133, 137, 138–139, 143

(*see also* nebari)

root ball 137, 138, 143

Sageretia 185

Sageretia theezans (*see* Sageretia)

sapwood *22*, 23

Satsuki Azalea *69*, 171

Scots Pine 120

seedlings, replanting 123

seeds 122, 123

Serissa 49, 186

Serissa foetida (*see* Serissa)

shari 146, 147, *150*, 151

Shimpaku (*see also* Juniper) 120

shohin (*see also* mame) 32

shoots 25, 27

soil (*see also* repotting) 110–111, 112, 137

sources of bonsai 131

open ground 134–141

South African Veld Fig 121

species 48, 63, 119, 120

hardy 160–175

tropical and subtropical 176–185

spruce 92, 147

Stuartia monodelpha (*see* Stuartia)

Stuartia 172

styles 36–39, 51

Broom 36

Cascade 37, 154–155

Classical 36–37

Clump 39

Double-trunk 39

Driftwood *30*, 31, 38, *147*, 148

Exposed Root 38

Forest 39

Formal Upright 36

Group Planting *33*

Informal Upright 36

Literati 32, 37, *42*, 43, 121

Nonclassical 37–39

Planted-in-rock 38

Raft 39, 158–159

Root-in-Rock *160*

Root-over-Rock 38, *20*

Semi-cascade 37, *118*, 119

Slanted 36, 156–157

Spiral Trunk 38

Upright *35*

Windswept 37, 120

Temperature 63

Temple Cedar 92, *93*, 164

tokonoma 40

tools 77–81

trace elements 66

training a young bonsai 128–130

Trident Maple 25, *26*, 63, 140–141, 161

trunk 22–24, 32, 33, 35, 51, 128, 133, 136, 144, 145, 152, 153

twig density 94–95

Ulmus parvifolia (*see* Chinese Elm)

Ulmus spp. (*see* Elm)

Watering 53–59

wire, types 97, *98*, *103*

wiring 51, 97–103, 128, 130

apex 100

branches 102–103

trunks 99–101

Wisteria 174

Xylem *22*, 23, 24

Yew 92

Zelkova serrata (*see* Japanese Grey-Bark Elm)

Zelkova sinica (*see* Chinese Elm)

▶ CREDITS AND ACKNOWLEDGEMENTS ◀

The publisher would like to thank Carl Morrow for his supportive guidance and his presence at the photo shoots. Lionel, Gail and Farrell Theron of Bishopsford Bonsai Nursery for their generosity in allowing us to take pictures in their nursery and their home. Mark and Gaby Wallance of Holistic Landscaping and John Thielmann, for their help and support. Sillery Nursery, and in particular, Bev Havenga, for her generous assistance. Rudi Adams for his generous help in preparing trees for our picture shoots and allowing us to shoot pictures at his nursery. Len Redfern and Norma Simons of the Oyama Bonsai Kai for their help and advice. Thanks also to the contributing photographers, Helmut, Michael, Peter, Claire, Walter and James, for their interest and support, and to the late Dan Lieberman.

KEY TO PHOTOGRAPHERS

Copyright rests with the following photographers and/or their agents: JS=James Smith; PB=Horizons West/Peter Bloomer; CL=Colin Lewis; CM=Carl Morrow; WP=Walter Paul; MP=Michael Persiano; HR=Ruger Bonsai Gallerie/Helmut Ruger; NHIL=New Holland Image Library/Claire McNulty.

KEY TO LOCATIONS

t=top; tl=top left; tc=top centre; tr=top right; c=centre; bl=bottom left; bc=bottom centre; br=bottom right; l=left; r=right; b=bottom; i=inset; bgi=background image.
No abbreviation is given for pages where there is a single image.

Page		Photo	Page		Photo	Page		Photo	Page		Photo	Page		Photo
1		CM	42		HR	72	l	HR	106-107		NHIL	151	t	MP
2		HR	43		NHIL	72	r	HR	108-109		NHIL	151	b	NHIL
4		HR	44		HR	73	t	HR	110		HR	152		CM
5		HR	45	l	CL	73	b	HR	111		HR	153		HR
6		HR	45	r	CL	74		HR	112		NHIL	154-159		CL
8		PB	46		HR	76		NHIL	113		HR	160		PB
10		HR	47		HR	78	t	NHIL	114		HR	161		PB
12		CL	48		HR	78	b	NHIL	115		HR	162		HR
13		HR	49	t	HR	79	t	NHIL	116		HR	163		WP
14		WP	49	c	HR	79	b	NHIL	117		HR	164		PB
15	t	HR	49	b	HR	80-81	t	NHIL	118		MP	165		HR
15	b	HR	50	t	NHIL	80	bl	NHIL	119		NHIL	166		PB
16		NHIL	50	b	HR	80	br	HR	120	t	HR	167		HR
17		NHIL	51	l	SIL	81	c	NHIL	120	b	WP	168		WP
19	t	NHIL	51	r	CL	83	tl	HR	121	l	NHIL	169		PB
19	b	HR	52		CM	83	bl	HR	121	r	WP	170		HR
20		HR	53		CM	83	r	CL	122		NHIL	171		PB
21		NHIL	55	l	HR	85		CL	124		NHIL	172		PB
23		HR	55	r	NHIL	87		HR	126		CM	173		PB
25		NHIL	57	t	HR	88	tl	CL	130		CM	174		HR
26		NHIL	57	b	NHIL	88	bl	CL	131		NHIL	175		HR
27	t	HR	59		HR	88	br	CM	132		NHIL	176		PB
27	b	CL	60-61		HR	89		MP	133		HR	177		WP
28		CL	62		CM	90		CL	134		NHIL	178		PB
29		NHIL	63		NHIL	91		CL	135		HR	179		NHIL
30		WP	64		WP	92		CL	138		MP	180		NHIL
31		NHIL	65		NHIL	93		HR	139		HR	181		NHIL
32		CL	66		NHIL	96		PB	140-141		CM	182		HR
33	t	CM	67		HR	97		NHIL	142		HR	183		HR
33	b	CM	68		HR	98		NHIL	145		CL	184		PB
35	l	NHIL	69		HR	99		JS	146		HR	185		HR
35	r	NHIL	70		HR	103	l	MP	147		CM	186		PB
40		HR	71	t	HR	103	r	HR	148		CM	187		NHIL
41		HR	71	b	HR	104		HR	150		WP			